INSIGHT COMPACT

MARTHA'S VINEYARD & NANTUCKET

GREAT LITTLE GUIDES

Compact Guide: Martha's Vineyard & Nantucket is the perfect on-the-spot guide to these perennially popular islands off the New England coast. It tells you all you need to know about their attractions, from the best beaches to the quaintest fishing villages, from state forests to Flying Horses.

This is one of more than 70 titles in *Apa Publications'* new series of pocket-sized, easy-to-use guidebooks intended for the independent-minded traveler. *Compact Guides* pride themselves on being up-to-date and authoritative. They are in essence travel encyclopedias in miniature, designed to be comprehensive yet portable, as well as readable and reliable.

Star Attractions

An instant reference to some of the islands' most popular tourist attractions to help you on your way.

Shenandoah p15

East Chop Lighthouse p19

Oak Bluffs p18

Flying Horses p20

Vineyard Museum p26

Chappaquiddick p30

Takemmy Farm p36

Jared Coffin House p49

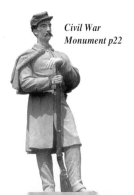

Civil War Monument p22

Old Mill p51

Cisco beach p59

MARTHA'S VINEYARD &NANTUCKET

Introduction

Places

Culture

Leisure

Practical Information

The Vineyard and Nantucket – Worlds Apart

Water defines an island. Whatever your mode of getting here, it means venturing at least a few miles over the Atlantic, whose expanse sets Martha's Vineyard and Nantucket off from coastal New England and the rest of the world. Life on the islands is shaped by the sea in every sense, creating an atmosphere of informality, individuality, freedom and escape.

Both islands offer a surprisingly varied balance of natural splendor, classic New England charm and up-to-the-minute casual elegance for the '90s. Most popular are the miles of beaches, undeveloped shoreline, cliffs and woodlands, where vacationers from all over the world come to sail, fish, swim and explore. In the fall, hikers and beachcombers share the islands with virtually every migrating species of bird on its way south. Lighthouses, farm houses and fishing villages all exude the bucolic and seafaring charm of 19th-century New England. Much of the architecture hasn't changed since the days when the whaling business spawned entire family fortunes and sailors' wives lingered at the widow's walk, awaiting their husbands' return. In the case of Oak Bluffs' Flying Horses, the nation's oldest carousel, historic architecture becomes something that you can ride on as well.

Sconset, Nantucket

Vineyard Haven

5

For decades both Nantucket and the Vineyard have also been a favorite retreat among the world's political, artistic and cultural elite. In recent years its visitors and residents have included everyone from the Clinton family, Princess Diana and Jackie Onassis to musicians such as Carly Simon and Billy Joel. The Vineyard tends to get a larger share of writers – novelists William Styron, John Updike, and Salman Rushdie have all come here – while Nantucket attracts artists, encouraging workshops, galleries and the Nantucket School of Design.

It is testimony to the islands' appeal that so many people find solace, excitement and fulfillment and peace along these idyllic shores, rolling moors and deep forests.

Location and landscape

Having broken the surface less than 10,000 years ago, Martha's Vineyard and Nantucket are geological youngsters. The glaciers which spawned them, however, date back much further. The Pleistocene Epoch, the time of the ice ages, occurred about 600,000 years ago, when glaciers from what is now Greenland and northern Canada began their painstaking migration south, dredging up millions of tons of sand, gravel and rock along the way. It wasn't until the fourth ice age, just 18,000 years ago, that the Laurentide Ice Sheet finally advanced

Gay Head

as far south as Cape Cod. When the ice crept back north, it left behind soil and sand in the form of the two islands.

Martha's Vineyard, the largest island in New England, lies about 5 miles (8km) south of Cape Cod. Shaped roughly like a triangle, with the peninsulas of Gay Head and Chappaquiddick affixed to two corners, it is 20 miles (32km) long and stretches over 100 square miles (26,000 hectares). It faces Vineyard Sound to the west, Nantucket Sound to the east, and the open Atlantic to the south. Although Chappaquiddick Island ('Chappy') is actually attached to the rest of the island by a long barrier beach to the south, this route requires an over-sand permit and most vehicles use the single-car ferry to cross from Edgartown.

The Vineyard is commonly broken up into 'up-island' and 'down-island,' referring to the degree of longitude as one travels west ('up') and east ('down'). Down-island includes the towns of Vineyard Haven, Oak Bluffs and Edgartown, while up-island begins in West Tisbury and spreads westward to include Chilmark, Menemsha and Gay Head. At the heart of the island, within the triangle formed by State Road, West Tisbury Road and Edgartown–Vineyard Haven Road, is the Duke's County airport and, around it, 4,000 acres (1,600 hectares) of undeveloped state forest.

Hikers delight in the Vineyard's diversity of terrain. Hillocks sweep upward from the shore, offering panoramas in every direction. At 308 feet (94 meters), Chilmark's Prospect Hill is the island's highest point, closely matched by Peaked Hill, where you can find the remains of the sandbagged signal corps outpost where lookouts watched for U-Boats in Vineyard Sound in World War II.

According to legend, the Indian god Moshup smoked tobacco planted on the Vineyard and, in tapping ashes from his 'fires,' created the island of Nantucket. But in reality this more distant island emerged from the same Laurentide Ice Sheet that created the Vineyard on its way down from Labrador. Located 30 miles (48km) off the Massachusetts coastline, Nantucket is about 15 miles (24km) long and scooped into a long, sea-smoothed curve to the north. Fringed by 55 miles (88km) of sandy beaches, the inland part of the island doesn't rise much more than 100 feet (30 meters) above sea level.

Unlike the decentralized population of the Vineyard, Nantucket has one main center – simply called Nantucket town – nestled into the harbor on the island's north shore. Open land sprawls outward to the south, west and east, where the rolling moors are covered with as much as 10,000 acres (4,000 hectares) of Nantucket's most famous flora, the heath family: cranberry, mealy plum and huckleberry. The huge Cranberry Bog at Gibbs Pond is a thriving business, and native cranberry products, jelly and preserves, are readily available in town.

Cranberry harvest

People and population

The islands undergo a dramatic population flux between summer and winter. The Vineyard has about 14,000 core residents, but by August the population swells far beyond 100,000, not counting day-trippers and weekend visitors. Nantucket's winter population is about half that of the Vineyard, approximately 7,000, but during the summer months that number may increase to 60,000 or more.

Even in winter, however, activity remains surprisingly energetic. Visitors are sometimes surprised to learn that both islands have full elementary and secondary schools, as well as college-level extension programs. Art and writing workshops continue throughout the winter, along with plays, musical performances and public readings at such year-round venues as the Vineyard's Wintertide Coffeehouse and the Old Whaling Church. In recent years, the promise of a winter retreat and off-season rates has brought a new generation of artists, craftsmen and writers to the islands as an oasis from city living.

Visitors are attracted by the miles of beach and sport fishing

Economy

Tourism replaced whaling to become the primary source of income for the islands in the late 19th century, nudged forward by increasing interest in sport fishing, the Vineyard's Methodist camp meetings, and the islands' first resort hotels. Real estate and the construction industry, in conjunction with the summer popularity of islands, also bolster the economies of both islands. Since then, resorts, restaurants, shops, tours and countless other service industries have sprung up in the wake of the islands' still-burgeoning success.

To this day, commercial fishing continues to provide many islanders with a vital year-round income. Local waters provide bluefish, scup and bonita, along with marlin, sailfish and black sea bass. Shellfish harvested on the islands include oysters, bay scallops, mussels, quahogs and steamers, and native islanders sell them to off-island distributors as well as local restaurants for year-round income.

Wildlife

Besides aquatic life, the islands' biospheres support a wide variety of animal life and vegetation, and islanders have made great strides in preserving the balance between nature and civilization. About 20 percent of the land on Martha's Vineyard is now protected against development, while a full third of Nantucket has been set aside in large tracts of preserved land.

Chappaquiddick Botanical Gardens

On the Vineyard, year-round wildlife areas offer such varied terrain as dunes, salt-marshes, woods, meadows and ponds. Deer, rabbit, fox, raccoon and fieldmouse all live here. Along the seashore, the changing tides unveil an ecosystem all their own. Horseshoe crab and a variety of shellfish feed well on the nutrients in the islands' salt marshes, and in turn provide ample food for the island's ubiquitous gull population, which most typically will drop the unsuspecting mollusks on roadbeds and rocks to crack their shells. Driving and hiking around the islands, it is not unusual to see a sea gull taking flight with a large, disoriented crab still squirming frantically in its beak.

Nantucket's seashore community is equally fecund, but there are not nearly as many woodland creatures inland. Not a single squirrel, chipmunk, or raccoon exists on Nantucket, although a local contingent of prairie dogs did live here until they were exterminated in 1900. Nantucket does have a large population of white-tailed deer, which began in 1922 when fishermen rescued one lone buck swimming several miles out at sea and brought him to the island, importing a pair of doe not long after. Now both islands allow deer-hunting to stabilize the white-tail population.

What the islands might lack in four-legged creatures is compensated for by wildfowl population. Virtually every type of bird migrating along the east coast stops on the island, including osprey, heron, plover, wild turkey, Canadian geese, snowy egrets, owls and marsh hawk.

Low-growing heath – bayberry, cranberry, beach plum, bearberry – sprawl across the moors of Nantucket and, to a lesser extent, the Vineyard. Nestled among the white pine, spruce and evergreen sprouts are the riot of wildflowers, shrubs and peat. As the woods give way to marsh and pond, wild rose and seaside goldenrod appear, along with the more autumnal sea lavender. Hikers heading into more rural regions up-island will also encounter congregations of tupelo or 'beetlebung' trees, so-called because early island settlers used its dense wood in making 'beetles' or mallets to drive corks into barrels – 'bungs.'

Whaling

In the early 1800s there was no more glorious or dangerous way for a young man to seek his fortune than aboard a ship leaving Edgartown or Nantucket Harbor to hunt the sperm whale. 'For every drop of oil, a drop of blood,' the whalemen's saying went, and all aboard the whaleship knew that they might as easily lose their lives as take home the 'greasy luck' of whaling profits.

The journey could be monotonous and then suddenly frantic. When a whale was spotted from the ship, oarsmen would set out in small boats to maneuver into the whale's circling range. Except the mate, who sat at the stern with the steering oar, no one spoke – one loud voice or even an errant ripple could send the whale 'galleying' below the surface at top speed. Worse, it could turn and smash

8

Canada geese

Nantucket meadow

Maritime memories

the boat, which was no larger than the mammal's tail, capsize it, or crush it and the crew in its jaws. If luck was with them, the man at the bow would plunge his 10-foot (3-meter) harpoon into the mammal's head, and with a cry of 'Stern all!' the chase was on.

A harpooned whale might 'sound,' or dive, and the men aboard would try to tie barrels to the mammal to track its reappearance at the surface. Or it might shoot forward across the surface with the boat behind it in what sailors called a 'Nantucket sleigh-ride,' which could last for minutes or hours. When the whale finally exhausted itself, the mate would take the bow and sink a lance into the vulnerable section of the head, severing its arteries, flooding its lungs with blood and killing it.

Thar she blows!

No matter how exhausting the chase, the real work had just begun. Towing the whale back to the ship, the men flensed its blubber and boiled it into oil which was stored in barrels below decks. From the whale's decapitated skull they baled out the waxy, pearly-white spermaceti, prized for manufacturing cosmetics and candles. Whalebone was saved for buggy whips and corsets-stays, and the sailors themselves found that polishing and engraving scrimshaw made good use of the whale's teeth as well as the long, empty hours of a multi-year voyage. Ironically, a sick whale could prove more valuable than a healthy one: its infections produced the morbid secretion ambergris, used as a perfume base all over the world.

Tools of the trade

At its peak, nearly half the world's whaling fleet sailed from the Vineyard and Nantucket. Their harbors flourished with warehouses, ropewalks, cooperages and forges. War disrupted the whaling trade – the American Revolution, and the War of 1812 – but after each of these conflicts whaling merchants only expanded their domain further, from the North Atlantic to the Pacific, and eventually to the Far East. Shops in Nantucket and the Vineyard traded in Indian spices, Oriental rugs and Chinese porcelain brought back from whaling ventures, displaying a truly cosmopolitan wealth of goods.

But by the mid-1800s, economic and social developments conspired to destroy the whaling industry almost completely. In Nantucket, two great fires, in 1838 and in 1846, wiped out the island's entire waterfront whaling operation. In 1859 petroleum was introduced to the market, replacing whale oil in the lamps of the world. The *coup de grâce* came with the Civil War, whose sea-battles destroyed most of the whaling fleets of both islands. Men seeking their fortunes began heading west in search of gold, and many families simply left for the mainland. Although agriculture and fishing continued, the islands would have to wait for the turn-of-the-century tourist boom before they would see such prosperity again.

Historical Highlights

Circa 8000BC Glacial ice begins melting, raising sea level and separating Martha's Vineyard and Nantucket from mainland.

2270BC First evidence of Native American camps. Wampanoag ('Easterners') called the Vineyard 'No-epe,' or 'Island in the Stream.'

1524 Italian navigator Giovanni da Vazzarrano sails past Martha's Vineyard, names it *Louisa*.

1602 British Captain Bartholomew Gosnold lands on Martha's Vineyard, Nantucket and the Elizabeth Islands, supposedly naming the islands after his daughters. Gosnold and his crew summer here, bartering with Indians for furs and skins, before returning to England in the fall.

1641 Bay Colony merchant Thomas Mayhew buys Martha's Vineyard, Nantucket and the Elizabeth Islands from two British noblemen for £40. The following year, his son Thomas Jr. begins Great Harbor, the first white settlement on the Vineyard, in what would later become Edgartown. The Mayhews establish a policy of fair exchange with Wampanoags, in which settlers do not take native land without their consent and proper payment.

1659 Tristam Coffin, a planter from Salisbury, Massachusetts, purchases Nantucket from Mayhew for £30. Attempting to escape the religious intolerance of Boston's Puritans, Coffin's fellow shareholders arrive on the island and meet with peaceful Algonquin natives there. Nantucket soon becomes a haven for the Society of Friends, or Quakers, led in monthly meetings by Mary Coffin Starbuck. Practicing personal freedom and pacifism, eschewing slavery and religious persecution, the Quakers's following grows on the island.

1712 Captain Christopher Hussey, blown out to sea, harpoons the first sperm whale off of Nantucket.

1723 Straight Wharf is built in the harbor of Nantucket.

1773 Three Nantucket ships returning to Boston Harbor with British tea are boarded during the Boston Tea Party, protesting British tea tax.

1775 American Revolution begins. Nathan Smith of the Vineyard arms his whaleship and captures the British schooner *Volante* in Vineyard Sound. Smith's attack may be the first naval battle of the Revolution.

1778 British fleet of 40 ships moves into Vineyard Haven harbor and raids the island's towns, burning shops and boats and taking cattle and sheep from the farms. The Vineyard has little defense against the raiders. Initially Nantucket attempts to remain neutral with the British, in part because of the Quaker committment to peace but also because the island relies heavily on British trade. Finally, however, they are drawn into the fray with the unfortunate result of losing the trust of both British abroad and Quakers at home.

1789 British whaleship *Emilia* rounds Cape Horn, opening the Pacific up to the post-Revolutionary whaling trade. Nantucket harpooner Archaelus Hammond spears the first sperm whale aboard the *Emilia*. Two years later the first Nantucket vessel *Beaver* rounds the Cape.

1812 Whaling trade disrupted by war. Islands' fleets are seized by French and British. Again the islands struggle to remain neutral, and again are mistrusted by both sides. Of Nantucket's 116 vessels, fewer than two dozen survive the war.

1818 Birth of astronomer Maria Mitchell on Nantucket. From early childhood Mitchell displayed a genius for the heavens as well as worldly philosophy – as a teenager she became the first librarian of the Nantucket Atheneum. At 29, standing on the roof of the bank her father ran, she discovered a comet which made her famous. She became the nation's first female college professor and the first woman admitted into the Academy of Arts and Sciences. In 1902, her relatives founded the Maria Mitchell Association to expand on her scientific discoveries, and pass on the love of science to new generations.

1820–30 Island whaleships begin venturing into profitable Japanese waters. Whaling industry reaches its golden age, and many of the beautiful captains houses on Nantucket and in Edgartown are built in this decade.

1828 First telegraph signals broadcast between Nantucket and Boston's South Shore, linked through the first East Chop Lighthouse on the Vineyard.

1835 First tents go up for Methodist camp meetings held in Oak Bluffs, formerly Cottage City. From 1835 to 1870, the 'campers' constructed platforms and support beams until the tents evolved into permanent cottages, closely nestled and colorfully painted. Gradually this 'carpenter's gothic' style gave way to massive 'Queen Anne'-style houses, with their spires and dormers, that tower around Oak Bluffs' Ocean Park.

1846 Fire along Nantucket's waterfront destroys over 300 buildings, a third of town. Several whaling merchants' fortunes are irrevocably ruined.

1847 Nantucket Atheneum constructed from a Federal-style design by island architect Frederick Brown Coleman. The Atheneum's inaugural address was given by Ralph Waldo Emerson. Its first librarian, 18-year-old Maria Mitchell, would later arrange for visits from such luminaries as Herman Melville, Frederick Douglass and John James Audubon.

1859–65 The commercial introduction of petroleum-based kerosene and the destruction of the islands' whaling fleets by Confederate ships mark the end of the whaling age. Martha's Vineyard begins to rely more heavily on agriculture, but both islands undergo deep depressions. Nantucket's population drops from 10,000 to 2,000 in the course of just a few years.

1870 Steamship service begins from New Bedford to Nantucket. Railroads begin advertising the islands as a vacation area. The first summer cottages are rented not long after.

1876 Flying Horses carousel, the oldest merry-go-round in America, is built in Cottage City, which will eventually become Oak Bluffs.

1879 Springfield, Mass., architect J.W. Hoyt builds the Trinity Park Tabernacle in Oak Bluffs campground. The Tabernacle now appears in the National Register of Historic Places as the largest wrought-iron and wood structure in America, topped with an unmistakable shining cross so that sailors at sea can find their way.

1895–8 Sea Captain Joshua Slocum sets sail from Martha's Vineyard and becomes the first man to sail alone around the world. Returning to the island, he publishes a bestselling account of the 46,000-mile journey, *Sailing Alone Around the World*. In 1909, he attempts to repeat his journey and disappears forever.

1909 Construction of Shearer House, the oldest African-American guest house on the island, completed in Oak Bluffs. In future years, guests would include Martin Luther King Jr., Adam Clayton Powell and Paul Robeson.

1914 Cape Cod canal completed, signalling a decline in commercial shipping activity in Vineyard Haven's harbor.

1956 The opulent Italian liner *Andrea Doria* sinks within a mile of the Nantucket Lightship after colliding in fog with the Swedish-American liner *Stockholm*. Fifty-two people die.

1966 Frank Sinatra and Mia Farrow honeymoon on the Vineyard; one of Sinatra's bodyguards drowns in Lake Tashmoo.

1969 US Senator Ted Kennedy drives off the Dyke Bridge after a party in Chappaquiddick, drowning his passenger, Mary Jo Kopeckne.

1974 Stephen Spielberg films *Jaws,* one of the top-grossing films of all time, on Martha's Vineyard. Island sculptor Travis Tuck assists with the set construction.

1981 Actor and comedian John Belushi is buried in Chilmark.

1993–4 President Bill Clinton and his family come to the Vineyard for their summer vacation, staying at Robert McNamara's former home in Edgartown.

Vineyard Haven harbor

Martha's Vineyard: Route 1

Vineyard Haven

Like most of the island, Vineyard Haven has taken different names throughout the centuries. Thomas Mayhew Jr. founded the first white settlement here in 1674, calling it Holmes Hole. 'Hole' refers to the harbor, while Holmes was probably the owner of the adjoining land. It was soon incorporated into the inland township of Tisbury, but as waterfront activity increased, the town built its own post office and took its current name in 1871. Legally and administratively, the town's name is Tisbury – but, on an everyday basis, Vineyard Haven is by far the more commonly used name.

For centuries the town's port has opened to the world. Seagoing commerce from Africa, the West Indies and Europe all stopped off at the town's harbor, and by the mid-1800s Vineyard Haven was second only to the English Channel in the volume of shipping, with over 13,000 vessels coming into port here. The opening of the Cape Cod canal in 1914, in combination with increasing use of overland transport, dramatically reduced the commercial traffic in the port.

The island's involvement in the American Revolution began here in 1778, when British ships moved into Vineyard Haven harbor, raided West Tisbury's farmlands and threatened to burn the town if islanders didn't turn over their livestock. It took a century for fate to make good on that threat, but in 1883 a terrible fire did sweep through downtown, wiping out 60 houses and clearing a path into the 20th century. Today Vineyard Haven remains the island's busiest year-round community, and the first town most visitors see as they step off the ferry.

Main Street café

Previous pages: Oak Bluffs

From the town's new Steamship Terminal, it's just a one-block walk up Union Street to ★★★ **Main Street** whose shops, cafes and summertime activity mingle effortlessly with the town's historical sites. A block to the left on Main Street is an impressive fieldstone ★ **National Bank** (tel: 693-9400) ❶, now Compass Bank. Once the site of Crocker's Harness Shop, where the fire of 1883 started, the current building was designed for Martha's Vineyard National Bank in 1905 by Boston architect J. William Beals. During the Great Depression, bank director Stephen Cary Luce offered personal backing for any islander who wanted to open a checking account, keeping the island's economy afloat. One of the town's two ATMs is located behind the main building.

A bank with a history

Leaving the bank and following Main Street to the left, turn left on Beach Road for a visit to the Martha's Vineyard **Chamber of Commerce**. Staffed by a friendly and informative crew of islanders, the chamber offers free visitors' guides, maps and up-to-the-minute tips about restaurant and hotel vacancies around the island.

Next door, at 15 Beach Road, offering a more historic view of local and regional culture, is the ★ **Bethel Maritime Collection** (tel: 693-9317) ❷. For more than a century, the bethel (Hebrew for 'House of God') was a sailors' hostel, and the gifts that its guests left here serve as the basis for this small exhibit. Admission is free, and the seamen's artifacts within give a brief history of the island through model ships, ivory carvings, seashells and historic photographs.

15

Wintertide Coffeehouse

Follow Beach Street to Five Corners and the **Wintertide Coffeehouse** (tel: 693-8830) ❸, whose non-profit commitment to folk, jazz and comedy improvisation crescendos in a national singer-songwriter workshop each fall. Stop by and pick up a schedule of their year-round events.

Beach Road Extension ends at the waterfront, and just beyond it is the 108-foot (33-meter) schooner ★ *Shenandoah* (tel: 693-1699) ❹. The ship is a fully-functional 1964 reproduction of the original, built in 1849, and in the summer months takes up to 26 passengers on extended cruises around the islands and eastern seaboard. The *Shen-*

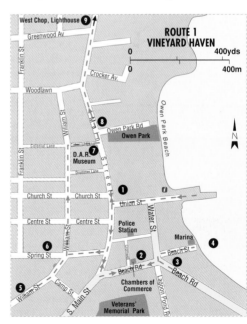

ROUTE 1
VINEYARD HAVEN

0   400yds
0   400m

West Chop, Lighthouse ❾
Greenwood Av
Franklin St
Crocker Av
Woodlawn
William St
Colonial Lane
Franklin St
Owen Park Rd ❽
Owen Park
Owen Park Beach
D.A.R. Museum ❼
Drummer Lane
Church St   Church St
Union St
Centre St   Centre St
Police Station
Water St
S. William St
Marina
Spring St ❻
Camp St
Wilfram St ❺
Beach Rd ❷
❸ Beach Rd
Chambers of Commerce
Lagoon Pond Rd
Veterans' Memorial Park
N

The Shenandoah

Captain Richard Luce House

Owen Park

andoah travels purely by wind power and is a frequent sight as it glides through Vineyard Sound.

Returning to the shop windows of Main Street, walk back to Spring Street and turn left for a block. Evidence of the harbor's halcyon days – the great Greek Revival houses erected by prosperous captains and shipping merchants – is in full regalia here on ★★ **William Street**. Half a block to the left on William sits one of the finest examples of Greek Revival, the **Captain Richard Luce House ❺**. Built in 1833, this massive yellow house set the standard for later captains' houses along William Street. Inspired and heavily influenced by the Parthenon, the porticos, Greek facades and famous columns dominated architecture during the island's most prosperous whaling years. You can tell Luce was a particularly successful captain.

Returning to the corner of Spring and William, turn left onto Spring Street. The second building on the right is Tisbury Town Hall, also called ★ **Association Hall** (tel: 696-4200) ❻. Built in the neoclassical style in 1844, the hall came into being as a church meetinghouse and eventually became the town hall. In 1971, to commemorate Vineyard Haven's tricentennial, actress and long-time island resident Katherine Cornell donated funds to remodel the theater on the second floor. Plays are still performed here in the summer months to great success.

Walk back to William Street and turn left. Two blocks up is Church Street, and its namesake, the stolid fieldstone Methodist Church on the corner, built in 1922. Continue on for another two blocks and look out for a tall white pole marking the ★ **Daughters of the American Revolution Museum ❼**. The schoolhouse building was first erected in 1829 as the first Tisbury School. It also served as the Congregational Church before the Congregationalists moved to Association Hall. The tiny museum, operated by the Martha's Vineyard Preservation Trust, retains some interesting whaling artifacts, and is open in the summer months, Monday through Friday. The Liberty Pole in front of it was placed here by the Daughters of the American Revolution. There is a plaque to commemorate – of all things – the three Revolution-era girls who used gunpowder to destroy the original pole, to prevent it from being used as a mast by British warships in 1776.

With its roofed gazebo and postcard-perfect view of the harbor, ★★ **Owen Park ❽** makes an excellent rest-stop for lunch or simply to step out of summer traffic on Main Street. The park is named after whaling captain William Barry Owen. Appropriately enough, it is perhaps the best point to observe the comings and goings of the port below. There are swings for children and the public beach is open to swimmers, although the chilly Atlantic water proba-

West Chop

bly won't prove tempting before mid-July. On alternate Sundays in summer, the town band holds concerts here.

About 2 miles (3km) beyond Owen Park, Main Street leads to **West Chop**, the island's northernmost headland, which helps cradle the entrance to Vineyard Haven's harbor. Here quaint cottages and classic Cape Cod-style houses mix with larger, more contemporary homes. Some might say the 19th-century rich were less ostentatious than their counterparts today, since they chose to wrap their summer homes in unpainted wood shingles. The island's first Methodist camp meetings began here in 1827 with the arrival of the New Hampshire itinerant preacher John Adams. Most of the Chop remained pastureland, however, until 1887, when private investors converted it into an upscale summer resort for vacationing Bostonians. To this day the Chop maintains a respected list of summer residents – novelist William Styron and columnist Art Buchwald own houses here, along with Mike Wallace of television's *60 Minutes*.

17

West Chop lighthouse

As the Chop tapers toward the sea, the ★★ **West Chop Lighthouse** ❾ comes into view. Like most of the lighthouses on the island, the West Chop light has been rebuilt numerous times throughout the years, first in wood in 1817 and later in brick in 1838. The effects of erosion on the 60-foot (18-meter) bluff forced its relocation twice, first in 1848 and again in 1891. In 1899 the red brick was painted its current white. The lighthouse is now fully automated (it was the island's last manned light), and Coast Guard personnel live in the lighthouse-keeper's quarters.

The road circles around at the lighthouse. If you wish to return to Vineyard Haven, turn right on Franklin, traveling past West Chop woods, an 83-acre (34-hectare) wildlife preserve maintained by the Sheriff's Meadow Foundation, and make your way back to town.

Oak Bluffs after dark

Route 2

Oak Bluffs

Religious revivalism swept the country throughout the 19th century, and in the town of Oak Bluffs, evangelical fervor was reviving more than the Holy Spirit. Methodist 'camp meetings' found a lasting home in Oak Bluffs – then called Wesleyan Grove – under the tutelage of Edgartown resident Jeremiah Pease. By its energetic and joyful nature, revivalism drew crowds from the start, and their tents soon clustered around the community's central meeting tent. Oftentimes whole families would set up a single tent with a sheet down the middle to divide the sexes.

Taking it easy

These happy pilgrims were the island's first summer visitors. Not coincidentally, the first 'meetings' were vacation-length, two-week affairs. By the 1870s, though, they were filling entire summers, just as the tents gradually transformed into Cottage City, a self-contained village of elaborate 'gingerbread gothic.' Today the residents own their cottages, but the land still belongs to the Camp Meeting Grounds Association, which rents it on a lot-by-lot basis.

The Carpenter Gothic style

By the Victorian era, Oak Bluffs was already a bona fide resort community, the island's first. Huge harborfront hotels sprung up along Lake Avenue and Circuit Avenue. At one point the Vineyard's only steam locomotive, the *Active*, ran from what is now the Oak Bluff's Steamship Terminal to the beach in Edgartown. In August 1869 residents strung Cottage City with hundreds of Japanese lanterns, beginning the annual summer tradition of Illumination Night – an event which has become so popular that its exact date is now kept secret until the last minute in order to deter crowds.

Oak Bluffs was also one of the first resort communities where African-American visitors were welcomed openly. As a result the town has become a summer favorite among the black community, who eventually began referring to the popular Oak Bluffs beach as the Inkwell. Harlem Renaissance author and Oak Bluffs resident Dorothy West wrote her recent novel *The Wedding* about this closely-knit community, and director Spike Lee keeps a summer home here as well.

The island's long-standing Portuguese community is also seated here in town. Having worked on whaling and merchant vessels from very early in the Vineyard's history, Portuguese-American islanders keep their own club grounds on Vineyard Avenue. Every July the club hosts a Celebration and Feast, complete with Portuguese cuisine, a parade and auction in celebration of their heritage.

From Vineyard Haven's harbor, Beach Road curves northeast past Lagoon Pond toward Oak Bluffs. Over the bridge is the island's hospital, and to the left, a group of oceanfront cottages sometimes called Eastville. Pirates occasionally lured schooners up onto these rocks, swinging lanterns on poles to give the impression of a safe harbor; the local sailors' term for these looters was 'mooncussers.'

Detouring to the right, follow Eastville Road to Country Road and turn right again on Shirley Avenue to visit the island's ★ **State Lobster Hatchery** (tel: 693-0060) ❶. Lobster is the most economically important species in these waters, and from its inception in 1949, the hatchery has studied hybridization and diet synthesis to preserve and enlarge the local lobster population. From these nationally-recognized laboratories, marine biologists stock about half a million bottom-crawling-stage lobsters annually to augment the natural population. In the summer there is an attendant on hand to answer questions, admission is free, and the habitat itself is open for visitors year-round.

Returning in the direction you came, turn back onto Beach Road and follow the signs to the right on Temahigan Avenue to **East Chop**. As a protective counterpart of West Chop, East Chop sweeps along a high bluff with a magnificent view of Nantucket Sound and Cape Cod. The impressive white and gray houses along the water are almost all seasonal homes – the furious winter wind off the ocean has been known to blow open barricaded doors – with only the occasional stalwart off-season tenants. To the right the road passes Crystal Lake, also called Ice House Pond because locals carved blocks of ice to keep food from spoiling before modern refrigeration techniques.

On the left, rising up from the 80-foot (24-meter) bluff, is the stately white ★★ **East Chop Lighthouse** ❷. The

State Lobster Hatchery

East Chop Lighthouse

first signal tower was built here on Telegraph Hill in 1802, and in 1875, rebuilt by the US government using cast-iron. Jonathan Grout Jr. established a semaphore-like system of ship-to-shore communication here in the first part of the 1800s. The lighthouse itself was painted white in 1988, before which it was a reddish-brown and sometimes called the Chocolate Lighthouse. Its observation platform is open on summer evenings, and in the past local musicians have climbed its spiral stairs with their mandolins and fiddles to accompany the sunsets.

Wesley Hotel

At the bottom of the bluff, Highland Drive hooks right past the East Chop Beach Club to Oak Bluffs Harbor and Lake Avenue. Turning left, Lake Avenue moves between Sunset lake and the harbor (once a single body of water called Squash Meadow Pond) past a long row of gingerbread cottages and the four-story, 82-room **Wesley Hotel** (tel: 693-6611) ❸ on the right. First constructed during the rococo heyday of 1879, the Wesley alone survived the fires that destroyed Oak Bluffs' wooden behemoths, but it wasn't for want of trying – in 1894 founder A.G. Wesley confessed to arson in an attempt to recoup lost funds. Since then the hotel has been renovated by more traditional techniques, most recently in the 1980s. The hotel is closed from October to May.

Cottage City Boardwalk

Facing Oak Bluffs Harbor directly to the south is an open-air collection of shops and fresh seafood stands contained in the **Cottage City Boardwalk** ❹. Perhaps the greatest allure here is the panoramic view of the harbor itself, which is maximized by the balconies and outdoor seating of such establishments as the two-story Cafe Luna. Boutiques within the faux-gingerbread mall has locally-made jewelry, crafts and clothing on display, and the Hy-Line ferry to the mainland departs from just down the dock.

Lake Avenue connects with Circuit Avenue at the town's busy traffic circle. Here you can find the enclosed ★★★ **Flying Horses Carousel** (tel: 693-9481) ❺ the oldest in the country. The 22 handcarved wooden horses, created for Coney Island in 1876 by sculptor C.W.F. Dare, were brought to the island

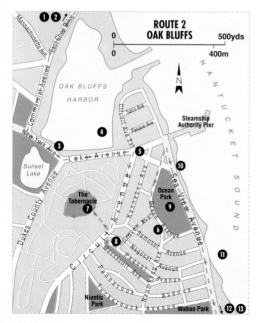

ROUTE 2
OAK BLUFFS

0 — 500yds
0 — 400m

OAK BLUFFS HARBOR

Massachusetts Ave
East Chop Drive
Commercial Avenue
New York Ave

Saco Ave
Pasque Ave
Circuit Ave East

Steamship Authority Pier

Lake Avenue

Sunset Lake

Dukes County Avenue

The Tabernacle

Ocean Park

Sea View Avenue

Samoset Avenue
Naushon Avenue
Pennacook Ave
Nashaquitsa Avenue
Pequot Ave

Niantic Park

Tuckernuck Avenue
Pennacook Avenue

Waban Park

N A N T U C K E T   S O U N D

The Flying Horses

via steamship in 1884. Now the carousel belongs to the island Preservation Trust, although it remains fully operational and a rainy-day favorite for children. Rides are still a dollar, with a free ride if you can grab a hanging brass ring as you pass it.

21

Visitors with cars may want to leave them at the parking circle before venturing to the right down ★★★ **Circuit Avenue**. Parking is scarce even in the winter down this busy, one-way street – sometimes called 'Circus Avenue' because of its frenetic July and August hum – and its individual shops and local color is best observed on foot. Because Oak Bluffs is one of the two towns on the island where liquor is sold (Edgartown is the other) there are three nightclubs in close proximity. The avenue's **Island Theater** (tel: 693-6450) along with the nearby Strand and Vineyard Haven's Capawok Theater, compose the oldest continuously running single-screen theater chain in the country. Every September, summer comes to an unofficial close here with Tivoli Day, whose festivities include a bicycle race and the Circuit Avenue Street Fair. The tradition began in the 1870s, when the town was still Wesleyan Grove, with a large roller rink, dance hall and popular song called the Tivoli (roughly 'I love it' spelled backward).

Circuit Avenue

So it was that 40 years after the first camp meeting, tens of thousands of summer visitors flocked to Wesleyan Grove to swim, hike and frolic in the sun. The Methodists, after attempting to ban peddling and further construction, finally erected a picket fence around their cottages. The enclosed area became ★★★ **Trinity Park Campgrounds** ❼. To reach the campgrounds, keep on the right side of the Avenue and watch for the sign marking the campground's main entrance. An open-air passage through the Arcade building leads directly to the ★★ **Trinity Park Tabernacle** (tel: 693-0525) constructed in 1879 to replace the original one-ton meeting tent. This open-air wrought-

Trinity Park Tabernacle

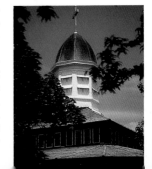

One of the 300 cottages

Ocean Park

Civil War Monument

iron structure, one of the country's largest, still hosts interdenominational worship services as well as community sing-alongs. Every year in August an All-Island Art Show and a Crafts and Collectibles Show are held by the Camp Ground Meeting Association. The Tabernacle itself seats more than 3,000 people, and large-scale musical performances in the past have included folk-rock star James Taylor and Bonnie Raitt.

The style of the campground itself, however, is anything but large-scale. Besides the impressive Methodist Church, the park is a cozy, fairy-tale network of narrow lanes and more than 300 brightly painted **Carpenter's Gothic cottages.** The original designers of these cottages used jigsaws to create their ornate scrollwork and cutouts, adding additional filigree, turrets and uniquely-shaped shingles on the high peaked roofs. Leaded cathedral windows and balconies complete the illusion of having stepped into another world.

Circling among the cottages, the park's walkway winds around the 1867 ★★ **Cottage Museum** (tel: 693-0525), whose open doors allow visitors a glimpse at the furniture, household fixtures and Methodist church artifacts of Cottage City from a century before.

Tabernacle Avenue leads back out of the campgrounds to Circuit Avenue. To the right is the ★ **Union Chapel** ❽, an octagonal building constructed in 1870, five years after the Civil War from which its name is derived. The Chapel's 96-foot (29-meter) spire tops its wooden domed ceiling, and the colorful woodwork and acoustics within make it an inviting temple of worship for the island's different religious denominations.

Behind the chapel and to the left is the green 7-acre (3-hectare) expanse of ★★★ **Ocean Park** ❾ and its gazebo in the center, with Nantucket Sound sprawling out beyond it. Band concerts draw huge crowds to the park throughout the summer. Bordering the park are some of the most impressive examples of Queen Anne style architecture, which consumed and expanded on the Carpenter Gothic revival of the mid-1800s. With their opulent turrets, sprawling porches and fish-scale shingles, these mansions represent the late-19th century arrival of wealth in Oak Bluffs and its logical extension on quaint gingerbread style.

The Episcopal Church is on the left of the park, and to the right is the town's ★ **Civil War Monument** ❿. The Monument was erected by a southerner who moved to the island. Inscribed with the message, 'The chasm is closed,' this lifelike statue of a Confederate Soldier is dedicated to the Vineyard's Union veterans, making it a unique addition to post-war reparations between North and South.

On the far side of Ocean Park, across Seaview Avenue, is the ★ **Oak Bluffs Public Beach** ⑪ which eventually becomes State Beach on the way to Edgartown. In the summer months the Oak Bluffs beach is packed with sunbathers and swimmers. This particular beach has become popular enough in the black community, and thousands come out each summer for the 'Inkwell's' buzzing social activity.

Oak Bluffs Public Beach

Seaview Avenue offers a 4-mile (6km) stretch of straight, paved 'boardwalk' along the Sound, ideal for cycling, walking or in-line skating. With the beach to the left, the path passes Waban Park and Farm Pond to the right before crossing over Veteran's Bridge. It's no surprise that one of the island's premier photographers, Allison Shaw, keeps her studio near the 8-acre (3-hectare) **Farm Pond Preserve** ⑫. The combination of pond grass, marsh and shoreline, owned by the Martha's Vineyard Land Bank, offers an unmistakably New England setting.

The Farm Neck Golf Course appears further down the road, offering its ocean view to those who come to play here. Recent guests have included Bill Clinton and the First Family.

23

As the road moves south toward Edgartown, the small inlet of ★★ **Sengekontacket Pond** ⑬ appears on the right. For the Wampanoag natives, who spoke a dialect of Algonquin, the name means 'bursting forth of tidal streams.' There is a scenic turnout on the left, and parking for those venturing out on either side for swimming or windsurfing. In midsummer it's common to spot sailboards gliding by on either side of the road. The pond is also a popular shellfishing spot for both humans and the constant flow of seagulls, which dip perilously between passing cars to scoop up the broken scallops and clams dropped on the roadbed.

Sengekontacket Pond

South Water Street

Route 3

Edgartown

The Vineyard's first white settlement began in Edgartown in 1642 under the auspices of Thomas Mayhew Jr. Its original name was Great Harbor, something of a misnomer in the very beginning. Lacking Tisbury Harbor's prime location or export base, Edgartown's little fishing and farming community grew slowly – 50 years after its initial settlement, there were still less than 40 houses in town.

Pedestrians welcome

At sea with attitude

Gradually, however, the advent of whaling in the 18th century brought an influx of activity, wealth and an upsurge of breathtaking architecture through Water Street and Summer Street. Whaling-related cordwainers, cooperages and foundries opened their doors on Dock Street. Stately Greek Revival captains' houses, replete with Doric and Ionic pillars, fanlights and widows' walks, rose up to overlook the harbor and Chappaquiddick Island on the other side. Portside activity increased further when whaleships from Nantucket began stocking up here, after realizing that a fully-provisioned ship couldn't get over the sand bar blocking Nantucket Harbor.

Eventually petroleum-based kerosene replaced whale oil in the lamps of the world, but Edgartown's economy suffered relatively little. Commercial fishing continued out of the shipyard, and the first resort hotels appeared in Katama in the late 1800s. The steam locomotive, and later a trolley, delivered bathers from Oak Bluffs to South Beach. Recreational sailing and yachting ushered Edgartown's tourism boom into the 20th century, and some of the island's finest and most historic inns are here, including the Daggett House and the Charlotte Inn. In the summer, its quaint downtown and sailboat-dotted harbor remain *de rigueur* stop-off for the global cognoscenti. Every July the Edgartown Regatta brings whole congregations of yachting clubs together, crowding the harbor with a riot of color and activity that is summer at its most ebullient.

Traveling toward Edgartown, Oak Bluffs Road intersects Edgartown-Vineyard Haven Road at the 'Triangle,' which houses the first of Edgartown's shops and restaurants. There is parking available here, with additional space at the Edgartown Grammar School. As in Oak Bluffs, you'll want to tour the downtown area on foot.

Past the triangle, keep right as the road becomes Main Street. Up ahead and to the left is the first and perhaps most palatial of the town's private houses, the ★★★ **Dr Daniel Fisher House** (tel: 627-8017) ❶ constructed at the height of whaling's success in 1840. If the island ever had a Renaissance man, Fisher might take the title: besides being the island's preeminent physician during his lifetime, he supposedly owned the largest spermaceti candle factory in the world and founded the Martha's Vineyard National Bank. His success is reflected vividly in this Federal style house. Its balustrade, porch, Greek Revival portico and cupola make it as much a pleasure from without as within. This is fortunate, because there are no tours available of the house, although it is made available by the Preservation Trust for public gatherings and parties.

Daniel Fisher House

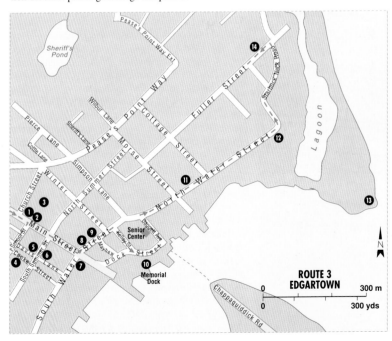

Old Whaling Church

Vincent House

The Vineyard Museum and the original lighthouse lens

Just past the Fisher House is the equally impressive ★★★ **Old Whaling Church** (tel: 627-8017) ❷ constructed in 1843 in the Greek Revival style by local architect Frederick Baylies Jr. Like the Fisher house, the church was constructed of high-quality pine shipped down from Maine. Six huge columns span the front portico, and the spiked tower shoots 92 feet (28 meters) into the air. Originally built for island Methodists, the church is now owned by the Preservation Trust. Although services are still held here, the 500-seat structure itself serves mainly as a community center for films, lectures and concerts, including the annual performance of Handel's *Messiah* at Christmas.

Behind the Fisher House and the Old Whaling Church is the ★★ **Vincent House** (tel: 627-8017) ❸. Unassuming among its towering neighbors, this full Cape farmhouse is generally thought to be the oldest house on the island, built around 1672. In 1977, the Preservation Trust moved the house from Mashacket Cove outside Edgartown on the South Shore, and restored it to its current condition. Such 17th-century construction techniques as wattle-and-daub clay insulation are visible in the walls. The Trust deliberately left the house mostly unfinished to display the common design motifs of its era, including a central chimney with three fireplaces. Tours of the house are available in the summer by reservation.

Continuing down Main Street, pass St. Elizabeth's Church and the Dukes County Court House, constructed of red brick in 1858 and refurbished almost a hundred years later. At School Street, turn left and walk three short blocks down to the ★★★ **Vineyard Museum** (tel: 627-4441) ❹. Here, filling an entire block at the corner of School and Cooke Streets, is the historic heart of the island. Maintained alongside the 1765 Thomas Cooke House, the Museum is run by the Dukes County Historical Society. Cooke was an Edgartown businessman and customs collector, and the house, a pre-Revolutionary Cape, is worth a look historically, having undergone no major changes since the 1850s. Out in front is the huge, original Fresnel lens for the old Gay Head Lighthouse. Designed in France for the 1856 lighthouse, the lens is mounted in a replica of the original watch house and lit at night.

The main house contains the **Francis Foster Museum** and **Gail Huntington Library of History**. The Museum has displays of scrimshaw, whaling artifacts and paintings, including one by Up-Island artist Thomas Hart Benton. The Library offers Revolutionary-era nautical charts and historic documents along with the largest collection of Vineyard-related books on the island. A nearby boathouse contains a Civil War-era fire engine, a whaleboat and

Boathouse, Vineyard Museum

various larger exhibits from the mid 1800s, along with a series of chicken tombstones by Nancy Luce, a 19th-century Chilmark eccentric.

The **Captain Francis Pease House** is the last of the major buildings on the block. An 1845 Greek Revival, this building exhibits very early Native American artifacts as well as housing an art gallery for Wampanoag pottery from the red clay of Gay Head.

27

From the Museum, take Cooke Street toward the waterfront and turn left on South Summer Street. Following South Summer to the left, you'll find the ★★ **Benjamin Smith House** (tel: 627-4311) ❺, built around 1760 for the Revolutionary War captain and now the offices for the 150-year-old *Vineyard Gazette*. The *Gazette*, which publishes bi-weekly throughout the summer and weekly in the winter, was owned and published by Vineyard legend Henry Beetle Hough and his wife until 1968, when he sold it to *New York Times* columnist James Reston. Reston's son Richard is now the publisher, and the offices – which have served as the island's poorhouse in their time – are open to visitors daily.

The Charlotte Inn

Just across from the *Gazette*'s offices is the renowned **Charlotte Inn** (tel: 627-4751) ❻, one of Edgartown's most charming diversions. The clapboard main house, which came into existence as a private residence for merchant Samuel Osborne in 1860, was transformed into an inn by his daughter Charlotte in the 1920s. The Edgartown Art Gallery is here on the first floor, resplendent with antiques as well as original paintings and prints, while the four other houses on the Inn's grounds offer a total of 26 individually-themed rooms and mahogany-furnished suites. Within the Charlotte Inn, for those who can afford it, is French cuisine comparable to the finest in Boston, at the enchanting L'Etoile.

Pagoda tree, South Water Street

Follow Main Street back down to South Water Street and look to the right. A massive pagoda tree spreads its limbs, the fully grown manifestation of a seedling brought over from China by Captain Thomas Milton after serving in the War of 1812. Milton's house, built in 1814, was eventually incorporated into the Harborside Inn. The tree is said to be the oldest on this continent.

The house beyond Milton's tree is the **Captain Valentine Pease House ❼**, now a private residence. Built between 1822 and 1836, the house came as a result of Pease's success with his whaleship *The Acushnet,* on which in 1841 Herman Melville had his only direct experience of whaling. Pease, supposedly, became Melville's model in creating the monomaniacal Captain Ahab in his 1851 novel *Moby Dick.*

The island's first tavern

Follow Water Street back to the left. The Edgartown shipyard is to your right, and there are more shops and restaurants on either side of North Water Street as well as the **Old Sculpin Gallery** (tel: 627-4881) ❽ on the corner of Dock Street and Daggett Avenue. The gallery, built for grain storage by Daniel Fisher, now includes works from the Martha's Vineyard Art Association and offers art classes.

Across from the gallery is the **Daggett House** (tel: 627-4600) ❾, whose historic Chimney Room was constructed as the island's first tavern by John Daggett in 1660. Daggett was summarily fined five shillings by the town for 'selling strong liquor.' The Inn itself was added in 1775. Since then, the structure has served as a sailors' hostel, a school, and a counting house. The original beehive fireplace has been incorporated into the cellar dining room, and a revolving bookcase hides a secret staircase which was probably built when the Inn was a custom house, to avoid taxes.

Old Sculpin Gallery

Daggett Street and Dock Street come together at the town dock, ★★ **Memorial Wharf** ❿. Originally owned by Daniel Fisher, who stored barrels of whale oil along Dock Street, the Wharf is home port for the town's fishing boats. On Memorial Day, schoolchildren parade down Main Street to the dock and throw flowers to honor islanders lost at sea. The small ferry to Chappaquiddick ('Chappy') leaves from here as well, carrying up to three cars along with whatever foot traffic comes aboard. Called the *On Time*, the small flatboat runs continuously and has no true schedule – the original got its name because its builder promised it 'on time' for the 1920 season. (For more information about touring Chappy, see pages 30–31).

The 'Chappy' ferry

Returning to North Water Street, follow the increasingly large captains' houses to the right. Between Morse Street and Cottage Street is the Federal-style ★ **Captain Jared Fisher House** ⓫, built for Captain George Lawrence in 1832. Notice its similarity to the Daniel Fisher House; both have Greek Revival porticos. On the roof stands a woman with a spyglass, looking out to sea. The house, owned by the Society for the Preservation of New England Antiquities, is closed to the public.

29

At the corner of North Water Street and Starbuck Neck Road is the 124-room **Harbor View Resort** (tel: 627-7000) ⓬, the largest hotel on the island. In 1891 the Harbor View was two separate buildings, but they've since been joined by a 300-foot (90-meter) veranda. Its ballroom and lavishly renovated interior (resort-chain Winthrop spent a reported $2 million to refurbish it) have made it a favorite spot for weddings and receptions.

Harbor View Resort

The hotel's front porch affords a stunning view of the Edgartown harbor, Chappaquiddick and the ★★ **Edgartown Lighthouse** ⓭. The original lighthouse, built in 1828, stood on a manmade granite island a quarter mile from the shore, and the only way to reach it was by boat. A year later, a wooden bridge was erected, called 'the Bridge of Sighs,' because of its popularity among young lovers. The 1828 structure was replaced 110 years later, on the same site. The bridge was replaced by a causeway, and eventually the ocean itself created the narrow sandy beach which now leads out to the current lighthouse.

Lighthouse beach

Follow Starbuck Neck around the bluff to the left to Fuller Street, which turns left back toward town. The second house on the left is ★ **Emily Post House** ⓮ and its attractive garden. Emily Post's presence on the island exerted a profound influence over Edgartown's social mores, lending the town much of its rarified character.

From downtown Edgartown, two interesting side-trips focus on the island's natural attractions. Although you may want to take your car to specific trailheads, much of the wildlife and vegetation is best seen on foot.

Swan Lake, Chappaquiddick

Cycling across Dyke Bridge

Brine's Pond Preserve

Chappaquiddick *See map on pages 34–5*

Chappy is the island's final frontier, unsettled by the white community until the mid-1800s. Wampanoag natives gave the island its name, which translates roughly into 'separated island.' In fact, this isn't true: a barrier beach connects with the Vineyard at Chappaquiddick's southernmost tip. The first houses were built during Edgartown's whaling days. By 1872, there were over 40 captains' houses on the island. To this day, though, the island remains largely undeveloped, its private land and miles of public beaches interrupted only by a single gas station, a beach club and a community center. There are paved roads, miles of hiking trails, and the Cape Pogue Wildlife Refuge and Wasque Preservation, as well as the rebuilt Dyke Bridge. But be advised: except for its sprawling beaches, much of Chappy's natural attractions require patience to find – from wild blueberries and huckleberries to the elusive piping plover, these details reward patience and perception.

From the ferry landing, travel straight ahead down Chappaquiddick Road to the sign for the Community Center. There is an entrance here to **Brine's Pond Preserve**, a 30-minute stop and a nice introduction to Chappy's biosphere. Follow the marked trail past Brine's Pond and the old windmill to your right. The trees here include pine, oak and beetlebung, the namesake for Chilmark's Beetlebung Corner. In the spring and summer, you'll find blueberries under the oak. Keep your eyes peeled for the shiny, pointed three-leaf of poison ivy underfoot. The trail eventually loops around the pond back to the entrance.

Continue along Chappaquiddick Road, following the unpaved stretch of Dyke Road. A third of a mile along on the left is ★ **Mytoi Japanese Garden** (tel: 693-7662). This is a serene 14-acre (5.5-hectare) park donated to the

Trustees by Chappy resident Mary Wakeman, landscaped into gentle hills by Hugh Jones. Azaleas and daffodils bloom here in the spring, and in the summer Japanese iris appear. Benches have been donated in memory of Chappy residents. An ornamental Zen-garden bridge arches over a pond with snapping turtles and goldfish, and birdwatchers may spot heron or marsh hawk in nearby marshland.

Dyke Bridge

Just down Dyke Road from the garden is the ★ **Dyke Bridge**, made famous by Senator Edward Kennedy's crash in 1969. The bridge is now completely rebuilt, and across it is the long beach of the 489-acre (198-hectare) ★★ **Cape Pogue Wildlife Refuge**. This stretch of beach alternates between ponds, tidal flats, marshes and occasional outcroppings of cedar. Vehicles venturing this far out must have beach permits, but the birdwatching is rewarding. Shore fisherman work these dunes in summer.

Fishing at Cape Pogue

At the far north tip of the Refuge is the island's most remote lighthouse, the ★★ **Cape Pogue Light**. Since its initial construction in 1801, the lighthouse has been destroyed by the sea and replaced no less than five times. The current structure, 55-feet (17-meter) high, was moved 300 feet (90 meters) back from shore by helicopter in 1985. Not far from the lighthouse, two picturesque fieldstone chimneys jut out of the eelgrass-covered bluff, the only reminder of the private homes washed away over the years. Pack a lunch, take pictures, and bring plenty of drinking water: this is a trek for serious hikers, a four-hour roundtrip unless you hitch a ride with one of the passing four-wheel-drive vehicles.

31

At the southernmost tip of Chappy is the 200-acre (81-hectare) ★★ **Wasque** (pronounced *Way-Squee*) **Reservation** (tel: 693-7662). More approachable and more popular than its northern counterpart, the reservation has a large parking lot and a $3 per person entrance fee. The dunes, ocean and bluefishing are the main attractions. A trail runs past Swan Pond, which originally connected Poucha Pond to the east and Katama Bay to the west. Fishermen from all over the Atlantic coast flock to Wasque Point for its convergence of currents, while swimmers prefer East Beach or Katama Beach. The walkways are designed to protect such delicate dune fauna as dusty miller and seaside goldenrod. The reservation is also prime habitat for thousands of waterfowl. Bring your binoculars.

Walking in Wasque

Felix Neck Wildlife Sanctuary See map on pages 34–5
Felix Neck (tel: 627-4850) provides 6 miles (10km) of marked trails through 350 acres (140 hectares) of inland woods, salt marshes and open meadow. Wampanoags farmed tobacco and squash here before the arrival of white settlers, and they called the area Weenomset, or 'Place

Felix Neck

of the Grape.' Felix Neck is now named after Felix Kuttashamaquat, one of these early Native American farmers. In 1969 private owner George Moffett donated the property to the Massachusetts Audubon Society.

One of the sanctuary's ongoing successes is the osprey, or fish hawk, endangered by DDT pesticide in the 1960s. Under the auspices of the Audubon Society, the osprey population is making a comeback. These large, flesh-eating predators resemble eagles, with an imposing wingspan that can stretch to six feet. They nest in dead trees near ponds and lakes, but local deforestation has necessitated strategic 'osprey poles' around the Vineyard. Felix Neck is embraced by Sengekontacket Pond on three sides, making it an ideal perching area for these birds.

Bird house

The reserve's entrance is clearly marked on the right side of the Edgartown-Vineyard Haven Road, about 2 miles (3km) northeast of the triangle. Park and walk to the ★★ **Visitors' Center**. Built on the foundation of a horse barn left over from earlier residents, the Visitors' Center offers trail maps, and interesting exhibits and aquariums. Nature walks are scheduled here throughout the year.

32

From the Center, follow the Orange Trail counterclockwise along the pond. To your left is the ★ **Waterfowl Pond** and observation blind. This is a marshy terrain, home for ducks, Canadian Geese and occasional long-legged herons. The Orange Trail eventually hooks up with the Red Trail. Follow this trail as it curves to the left. Across Sengekontacket is **Sarson's Island** nesting area for the island's cormorants. These are darker than seagulls, and have a distinctly longer neck, with a pouch underneath it for holding captured fish.

Canada geese

Follow the Red Trail to manmade Elizabeth's Pond on the right, and turn right on the Yellow Trail. The old building on the right was once a hermitage for resident Clarence Smith, and now is headquarters for the Reservation's Fern and Feather Day Camp. Further along, Edgartown's **State Beach** comes into view, the narrow barrier which divides Sengekontacket from the Atlantic. Don't be surprised by windsurfers or shellfishermen in the pond – these waters are seeded for scallops and clams, and the calmer sea breezes provide a training ground for sailboards.

Where the Yellow Trail meets the pond's edge, turn left onto Shad Trail. Shadbushes (also known as juneberries after the month in which they bear fruit) sprout along this trail. Follow this trail south along the pond to ★ **Majors Cove**. Along with the plethora of shellfish and finfish here you may find the empty shell of the horseshoe crab, a prehistoric hold-out from the island's glacial origin in the Pleistocene Era. Follow Shad Trail until it intersects with the Yellow Trail again and turn right to return to the Visitors' Center.

Route 4

West Tisbury/North Tisbury

Incorporated in 1671, West Tisbury and North Tisbury cut a wide, rural swath down the middle of the island. These gently rolling hills, sometimes looking more like New Zealand than New England, were created by the terminal moraine left over from glacier activity. The area's sheep and dairy farms have formed a strong agricultural backbone for the island since its first settlement, compensating for the town's lack of waterfront exposure, and fresh produce stands, grazing sheep and miles of rambling fieldstone walls evoke bucolic New England charm.

Summer blooms

Most of the residents are year-round, their homes oftentimes tucked back on private roads with long, unmarked driveways. The captains' houses of Music Street, however, offer a renegade infusion of waterfront architecture – sometimes literally, in the case of the original 1817 West Chop lighthouse keeper's quarters, which was transplanted to West Tisbury when erosion forced its relocation. The street itself was named from the years when the captains who owned these houses brought in imported pianos, and Sunday afternoons were full of mingling music. Historian and author David McCullough keeps a year-round home here and has occasionally hosted PBS documentary specials from his porch. West Tisbury is also a home away from home for film director Mike Nichols and his wife Diane Sawyer, as well as providing a hometown for fictional FBI Agent Fox Mulder in television's *X-Files*.

33

From Vineyard Haven, follow State Road southwest past the shops and businesses on the outskirts of downtown. To the right, a scenic turnout marks the ★★ **Lake Tashmoo Overlook** and beyond it, Vineyard Sound and the

Lake Tashmoo Overlook

Elizabeth Islands. The Wampanoag name Tashmoo means 'great spring,' from the days when the opening to the Sound was just a creek. Native fishermen seined the creek for herring before it was dredged to allow boat traffic through, and Lake Tashmoo now provides private long-term mooring as well as the picturesque roadside view.

State Road continues past ★★ **Chicama Vineyards** (tel: 693-0309), the island's one vineyard and the first licensed winery in Massachusetts. Turn left onto Stoney Hill Road and follow it to the vineyard, where former San Franciscans George and Catherine Matheisen produce more the 8,000 cases of wine annually. Besides more than a dozen varieties of local wine, they also offer herb vinegars, jams and jellies. Wine tastings go on year-round, and a tour is offered in the summer months.

★ **Thimble Farm** (tel: 693-6396) on Stoney Hill invites visitors to pick their own fresh strawberries and raspberries in season, and sells fresh flowers and produce from their huge greenhouses.

Chicama Vineyard

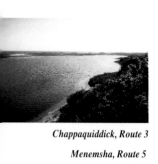

Chappaquiddick, Route 3

Menemsha, Route 5

Veer right where State Road forks away from Old County Road, then turn right onto Indian Hill Road. Follow the sign at the crossroads straight ahead to see what remains of an ancient island settlement known as ★ **Christiantown**. Before it was Tisbury, the farming community here was called Takemmy (Wampanoag meaning: 'Where anybody goes to grind corn'), and in 1659 the local government allotted one square mile of land to local missionaries to convert natives to Christianity. The Christiantown Meeting House was erected here in 1829, and it stands complete with six pews and a pulpit inside. Nearby tombstones mark an Indian graveyard, and a footpath beyond the stones leads to an observation tower overlooking the area.

Return to Indian Hill Road and continue to the right to explore ★★ **Cedar Tree Neck Sanctuary**. One of the most eclectic examples of different island ecosystems, this 250-acre (100-hectare) property leads between two sassafras trees through forested areas, ponds and down to the

Christiantown memorial

Cedar Tree Neck

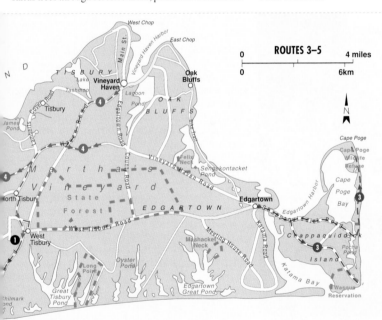

ROUTES 3–5

Takemmy Farm residents

beach and Vineyard Sound. There are three color-coded trails, the red leading most directly to the beach, the white and yellow looping down to the south. Lookouts have been cleared periodically to allow a clear view of the water, the Elizabeth Islands and the Cape beyond it.

Drive back to State Road the way you came and turn right toward North Tisbury. To the right, the animals you'll see grazing under the willows aren't horses but llamas: they belong to Frank and Mary Bailey's ★★ **Takemmy Farm** (tel: 693-2486). Llamas are child-friendly for petting, and the farm, actually a fully-operational ranch, raises the animals for farm labor and llama wool. Hand-knit sweaters are available for sale. The Baileys' farm features a 300-year-old farmhouse with antique-appointed guest quarters for more curious visitors.

The giant oak

Where State Road joins North Road is a **giant oak** with serpentine arms squirming off in every direction. The late Alfred Eisenstaedt, *Life* photographer and island resident, immortalized the oak on film in 1969. Since then the wind has torn off some of its heavier branches, but the tree itself remains an island landmark for amatuer photographers and islanders alike. Park the car and walk back along the road to the tiny collection of shops. Nearby is Goffs' Gallery & Bookstore and Martha's Vineyard Glassworks, where visitors can watch as local craftsmen blow glasses and pitchers in the hotshop. Across from the Glassworks is up-island's response to the Black Dog, the gourmet Red Cat restaurant.

State Road becomes South Road here and leads southwest into the heart of West Tisbury. To your right across an open field is the Vineyard's new ★ **Agricultural Hall**. The hall is a New Hampshire barn that was taken apart, transported and reassembled here in the summer of 1995.

Celebrated island sculptor Travis Tuck provided the new cow weathervane. In September 1995, musicians Carly Simon and James Taylor performed together for the first time in years at Livestock '95, a fund-raising event held to mark the inauguration of the new hall. The Agricultural Fair, an annual fete dating back 130 years, is held here in August.

At the Agricultural Hall, turn left from South Road onto Scotchman's Lane and follow it over to Old County Road – the location of the ★★ **Granary Gallery** at the Red Barn Emporium (tel: 693-0455, 800-472-6279). Alfred Eisenstaedt's photography hangs here, showing his sharp eye for Vineyard landscape as well as off-island subjects. The gallery also displays the work of island photographer Allison Shaw, and there is a room of McAdoo hooked wool rugs, an island craft. New exhibitions appear on Sunday nights, and these openings always prove to be popular events.

Granary Gallery

Turn left after the gallery on Old County Road to the West Tisbury-Edgartown Road, and left again. On the left side of the road is **Old Mill Pond**, the West Tisbury Police Department and the Martha's Vineyard Garden Club, headquartered in the old mill itself. When it was still operational in the 19th century, the factory turned out a thick wool fabric called satinet for sailors' pea coats. Now the pond is home for much of the up-island duck and swan population, and picnic tables make it an ideal lunchbreak oasis.

Past the pond, just beyond the fire department sign, on the same side of the road, is the privately-owned **Joshua Slocum House**. Built in the early 18th century, this unassuming Cape house with a bronze plaque is set on a small bluff. Slocum moved in after sailing his 36-foot (11-meter) schooner *Spray* single-handedly around the world, and added an additional wing to the house modelled after Robert Louis Stevenson's house in Samoa. Here he wrote a bestselling account of his journey and attempted to settle into a life of farming. Restlessness eventually drove him to retrieve the *Spray* from its moorings in Menemsha, however, and in 1909 he set out for the sea, never to be seen again.

Turn around and take West Tisbury-Edgartown Road to the intersection with South Road, following it left into 'downtown' West Tisbury. Park the car along the roadside: this cozily arranged area is best perused on foot, beginning with ★★ **Alley's General Store** (tel: 693-0088). Alley's, which boasts that it has been 'dealers in almost everything' since 1858, was recently restored by an island architecture firm with the assistance of celebrated locals such as David McCullough. This quintessential store, with

Alley's General Store

its front bulletin board invariably covered with announcements for local happenings, sums up the community spirit of West Tisbury more succinctly than any other single building.

Next to Alley's is the 1673 West Tisbury ★★ **Congregational Church** (tel: 693-2842) with its classic white facade and New England steeple. A replica of this church is said to have been built in Samoa, thanks to Joshua Slocum's influence on his trek around the globe.

Across the street from the church is the ★★★ **Field Gallery and Sculpture Garden** (tel: 693-5595) ❶, the work of island sculptor Tom Maley. Maley's imaginative menagerie of cubistic and Botticellian *bon vivants* can be spotted all around the Vineyard, but the garden is the largest collection of his creations. The gallery, which was built in 1971, has exhibits during the summer of local artists, including *Village Voice* cartoonist and seasonal resident Jules Feiffer.

At the corner of Music Street and South Road, the three-story ★ **town hall**, with its mansard roof and distinctive arrangement of dormers, once served for a time as the Dukes County Academy and then as the local schoolhouse. Next to it is the town's **old Agricultural Hall** (tel: 693-0100), where the largest grossing Farmers' Market in the state is still held on Saturdays from 9am to noon. There's a vast array of fresh produce and dairy goods, plus locally baked food and homemade pesto.

For an appropriate end to the West Tisbury tour, return to your car and drive north on State Road to the West Tisbury **cemetery**. Here lie buried some of the Vineyard's most seminal names – Mayhew, Pease and Slocum, as well as the 19th-century eccentric Nancy Luce, whose tombstone is adorned with plastic chickens and roosters to commemorate her beloved pet birds.

38

Sculpture Garden

Route 5

Up-Island *See map on pages 34–5*

Beyond West Tisbury, the island, though narrowing, somehow seems to expand, at least until that first glimpse of blue ocean. The hilly expanse of shoreline and meadow known as 'up-island' consists of three distinct areas: the town of Chilmark, the fishing village of Menemsha, which serves as Chilmark's port, and the Wampanoag township of Gay Head. Among them are two exceptional wildlife preserves, including the two highest points on the island, and the National Landmark red clay cliffs, whose geology has offered some of the glaciers' most revealing history.

Gay Head Cliffs

The town of Chilmark was incorporated in 1694 and began as a fishing and farming community. Sheep and other livestock roamed the hills, which were communally owned and managed on a feudal system. Unlike the waterfront areas of Tisbury and Edgartown, Chilmark's residents built their houses at a generous distance from one another, and for years the combination of inexpensive property and evocative natural settings encouraged an influx of writers and artists including Missouri-born Thomas Hart Benton and Jackson Pollock. Ironically, real estate in Chilmark now is among the most expensive on the island, but most of it remains blessedly undeveloped.

Menemsha Pond

Menemsha is the island's last fishing village. Its harbor was created in 1905, when the creek leading into Menemsha Pond was dredged and fortified with rock or 'riprapped' to allow the passage of fishing boats. In the 19th century, the stretch of shoreline southwest of the harbor, called Lobsterville, brought in lobstermen, trap fishermen and handliners, and their fishing shacks, hanging with nets and traps, lined the shoreline. Now Lobsterville is a beach with a bicycle ferry spanning the harbor. On the Menemsha side, the beaches, wharfside shops and shoreline restaurants have made the waterfront as popular with tourists and photographers as fishermen.

Although it's not referred to as an island, the 3,400-acre (1,375-hectare) peninsula of Gay Head is scarcely more connected to the rest of the Vineyard than Chappaquiddick is. A single causeway allows South Road to enter the township on the way to the 150-foot (45-meter) cliffs at the far west end of the island. The Wampanoags have lived here for 5,000 years and still maintain ownership of the cliffs, via a $4.5 million, 475-acre (192-hectare) land buyback in 1987. Incorporated in 1870, the town was long known as Aquinnah, meaning 'long-end' or 'high-land.' The natives here, like the white settlers, were primarily fishermen and farmers, and often served as harpooners on whaling ventures as immortalized by Melville's Gay

Chilmark Cemetery

Header Tashtego in *Moby Dick*. Amos Smalley, another Wampanoag harpooner, was the only islander to spear a white whale.

Follow South Road from West Tisbury southwest along the ponds, moors and ocean views into Chilmark. At the top of Abel's Hill, turn right into the ★ **Chilmark Cemetery**. A monument describes Thomas Mayhew Jr., founder of Edgartown, preaching to natives here in 1657 before venturing out on his 'ill-fated' trip back to England. This is also the site of Chilmark's first meeting house, built in 1701 and now long gone. Playwright Lillian Hellman is buried here, and John Belushi's simple stone (sometimes adorned with a beer can memorial) is set up in front. The body itself is buried in a undisclosed plot.

Continue along South Road, past the Chilmark Community Center and the bank, to Beetlebung Corner. The Chilmark Police Station is at the intersection, next to the town's war memorial. Turn right onto Menemsha Cross Road and follow it to North Road. Menemsha Harbor is to your left, and to the right, a mile up North Road, brings you to the ★★ **Menemsha Hills Reservation**. Fifteen thousand years ago the last of the Hudson Bay ice sheets left these hills scattered with clay, gravel, sand and boulder, causing a variety of moistures levels – bogs and brooks appear in the low valleys, and oaks spring up as the incline grows sharper. Amateur botanists will find bearberry, lichen and false heather along the reservation's two trails, as well as red maple, beech and beetlebung trees.

Menemsha Hills

The trails are both loops and involve some uphill hiking. Harris Trail is a one-mile round trip which winds up at the top of **Prospect Hill** with a spectacular view of the Cape and Elizabeth Islands. From the peak, hikers can continue on Upper Trail to the great sand cliffs on the north shore of the island, an additional 2-mile (3km) round trip. Along the rocky shoreline is a historic brick factory along Roaring Brook. Maps for the trails are posted near the reservation's parking area, along with a check-in book.

Leaving the reservation's parking area, turn right onto North Road again and follow it for a mile to Menemsha Harbor and ★★★ **Dutcher Dock** ❷. Widely considered to offer the island's best sunset, Menemsha has an excellent beach, its own post office, quaint shops and fresh seafood, both take-out and eat-in. Its wharf is home for the up-island commercial fishing fleet, and there are hookups for temporary visitors as well. The island's Coast Guard station is the most prominent building, but the wharf's sun-faded boathouses are certainly the most picturesque. When Steven Spielberg needed an authentic New England fishing village to terrorize in *Jaws,* he set up his cameras here and left behind the sharkhunters' boat *Orca* on the beach, where it lies to this day.

Commercial tackle

Take Menemsha Cross Road back to Beetlebung Corner and turn right onto South Road again. Chilmark's ★ **schoolhouse** – built in 1860 and only recently expanded from one room to two – is on the right. Chilmark Chocolates and acclaimed eatery Feast are next door, alongside the spired **Methodist Church**. The church was relocated from Edgartown to Middle Road and, in 1915, to its current location, where island carpenter Roger Allen added the steeple.

Crossing the causeway into Gay Head, South Road maneuvers past some of up-island's prettiest views. Modern architecture mingles with older houses along the hills and stone walls of ★★ **Menemsha Pond**, which offers two breathtaking water-views with one glance – the pond, and the Sound behind it. Passing between Menemsha Pond and Squibnocket Pond, the road crosses Herring Creek, named from the mini-industry it spawned. For years islanders seined herring here, smoked, salted and pickled them, exported them and used them for lobster bait.

Menemsha Pond

Facing Menemsha Pond at the creek is the cottage first rented by American Regionalist Thomas Hart Benton in 1920, for $25 a summer. For 55 years, Benton came back to the house with his family, and his work is displayed at the Vineyard Museum, Edgartown. The Modernist Jackson Pollack, a protégé of Benton's, visited in the 1930s, staying in a nearby chicken coop called 'Jack's Shack.'

41

From South Road, Gay Head appears as a cluster of houses, the fire department, and a former one-room schoolhouse on the left, now the village's library. Behind the library is the Congregational Church, overlooking the Atlantic. Founded in the 1700s, it is the old Indian Baptist Church in North America. For a closer view of the Gay Head beach, turn left on ★★ **Moshup's Trail**, the scenic drive leading up to the cliffs. The road was named after the Wampoag giant Moshup, who is thought to have laid down the rocky shelf of Devil's Bridge so that he could walk out to Cuttyhunk at the far tip of the Elizabeth Islands, but left the project unfinished. Legend has it that Moshup roasted and consumed whole whales and cast the ashes to form the island of Nantucket.

Traditionally, the island-based Wampanoag tribe has remained self-reliant and industrious through its own merits. The federally-recognized Tribal Council, which consists of an elected chairperson and 10 Council members, meets at the new multi-purpose building erected in 1994. The Tribal rolls list over 700 members, 300 of whom live on the Vineyard with the others residing all over the US.

Moshup's Trail meets up with South Road again at the ★★★ **Gay Head Cliffs** ❸. For sailors returning from the sea, these magnificent reddish-orange clay embank-

Gay Head Cliffs

ments were the first sign they were home, thus giving Gay Head its 'gaiety.' Shops and seafood stands have popped up along the walkway to the cliffs, but the view from the observation platform justifies all the fuss, particularly toward late afternoon when the cliffs' colors are at their most vibrant. The first settlers used the clay to paint their houses and pave their roads, and later bathed in it for its restorative effects, but efforts to curtail erosion now punish any such tampering. In the past, archaeological exploration through the different layers of clay has yielded 100 million years of prehistory, from arrowheads to whale and shark fossils. The partial skeleton of a camel was also recovered here – roughly 12,000 years after it became extinct in North America.

Looking out to sea, the only land mass between here and the Bahamas is **Noman's Land**, a tiny island used by the government as a naval bombing target. In the 1800s, however, the island was a seasonal and even year-round home for a few Vineyard families, who fished and raised sheep there. Late in the 19th century, up to 60 boats sailed out of Noman's Land. Conservationists hope to someday convert it into a nature preserve.

Gay Head Lighthouse

Beyond the cliffs is the 1844 ★★ **Gay Head Lighthouse**, the only brick lighthouse left on the island. In its first incarnation, in 1799, the lighthouse was built of wood and had one of the country's first revolving lights. Cold and dampness caused the wood to swell up, leaving the lighthouse keeper and his wife to crank the light by hand. In 1856, the innovative new Fresnel lens was installed, after being exhibited at the World's Fair in Paris. The lens, composed of 1,009 smaller lenses, foreshortened the beam's focal length and intensified the light dramatically. It has since been replaced and is exhibited in the Vineyard Museum.

In January 1884, the worst shipwreck in the island's history occurred on the sunken reef off Gay Head when a steamship bound for Savannah struck the glacial boulders. A Humane Society boat with Wampanoag mariners on board was able to reach the vessel from Gay Head, but not before 122 passengers died in the freezing Atlantic.

Outermost Inn

Coming out of the parking area at the cliffs, turn right onto Lighthouse Road. From here every porch has a spectacular waterview, including the sprawling, gray-shingled **Outermost Inn** (tel: 645-3511). Although young by Vineyard standards (it was built in 1971), the Inn and its adjoining restaurant maintain a classic, hardwood simplicity that fits in with the natural splendor of its 35-acre (14-hectare) dune-and-shoreline environs. The owners are Jean and Hugh Taylor, relatives of the folk-rock musician James Taylor, and the musical instruments around the inn bespeak its musical pedigree.

Follow Lighthouse Road around the gentle curve of shoreline to ★ **Lobsterville Beach**. The sand here is pebbly and slightly rougher on bare feet, but the view across the Sound is unforgettable. The five Elizabeth Islands spread across the surface of the water: from the left, they are Cuttyhunk, Nashawena, Pasque, Naushon (the largest), and Nomanesset. In the 19th century fishermen spent six months of the year on these islands, most of which are privately owned now and largely unpopulated. The bicycle ferry from Menemsha lets out here, but otherwise the trip across the harbor is deceptively lengthy, leading around to Gay Head and South Road.

Lobsterville Beach

Follow South Road from Gay Head to Beetlebung Corner and continue straight ahead on Middle Road. A mile along, marked by a 'GO SLOW' sign on the right side of the road, is the entrance to ★★ **Peaked Hill Reservation** and the highest point on the island. Worn-out hikers needn't worry: this is all driving, and the narrow, paved road runs straight to the top, where Peaked Hill enthusiasts have stacked six feet of boulders to insure that its 311-foot (95-meter) height overshadows nearby Prospect Hill.

For those with the energy for exploring, the Reservation offers 70 acres (28 hectares) with five different trails leading around such landmarks as Wee Devil's Bed and Stonecutter's Rock. The sandbagged remains of a World War II signal installation rest just a few yards from the parking area. There are 150 varieties of plant life and 50 types of birds, including the ground-nesting killdeer and American woodcock. Hikers should watch their step in hatching season, and also beware of the island's deertick population, whose bite can cause Lyme disease.

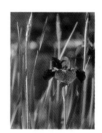

Springtime iris

Follow Middle Road to its intersection with Music Street in West Tisbury and turn right into town, concluding the tour of up-island.

Replicating the Bounty,
Nantucket harbor

Nantucket: Route 6

Downtown Nantucket

In 1962, Nantucket's waterfront area was refurbished by Walter Beinecke Jr., complete with replica gaslights and freshly landscaped terrain. The result, upon stepping off the ferry at Steamship Wharf, is a seamless amalgam of authentic cottages and perfectly constructed reproductions. Like the waterfront communities of the Vineyard, these closely nestled boathouses, piers and whaling-era architecture are best seen by foot.

Begin the tour by turning left on Easy Street, which connects the **Five Wharfs**. Though Old North Wharf is privately owned, Straight Wharf offers an introductory meal and waterview at two established restaurants: Rope Walk (tel: 228-8886) and the Straight Wharf Restaurant (tel: 228-4499). Further down, Old South and Commercial Wharf have galleries, shops and rental cottages for yachters.

At the head of Straight Wharf, the ★★ **Museum of Nantucket History** (tel: 228-3889) ❶ stands in the brick warehouse constructed for Thomas Macy following the great fire of 1846. Whaling artifacts, an antique fire engine and a 13-foot (4-meter) diorama of 18th-century Nantucket are displayed inside. The museum is most valuable as an initial historic overview. Buy a museum pass here for all the Nantucket Historical Association's exhibits.

Main Street

Previous pages:
Old-style shopping

From Straight Wharf follow Main Street to its intersection with South Water Street. The pillared, three-story brick house at Main Street Square is the ★ **Pacific Club** (tel: 228-3643) ❷ owned in 1772 by shipping merchant William Rotch and originally used as his counting house.

Rotch's life crossed paths with history more than once: he owned the *Beaver* and the *Dartmouth,* whose holds were raided of British tea during the Boston Tea Party. The *Beaver* later became the first American whaler to round the Cape, and the *Dartmouth* was the first into a British port after the Revolution. Rotch also defended a slave named Boston, after Boston's master attempted to take the man's whaling wages, and ended up getting him freed – a characteristic illustration of Nantucket Quaker emancipation. In 1789 Rotch's warehouse became one of the country's first Custom Houses, and in 1861 a group of shipmasters bought the property as an exclusive club. The club survives, its exclusivity does not; the island's Chamber of Commerce occupies the upper floors.

From the square, turn right on South Water past the **Dreamland Theatre** (tel: 228-5356) ❸ which began life in the mid-1800s as the Main Street Quaker meeting house, at the time the largest structure in town. It was transplanted to Brant Point for use in the Nantucket Hotel, and finally floated across the harbor in 1905 to become Nantucket's first movie house. First-run films in the summer make this an essential rainy-day stop.

Dreamland Theatre

47

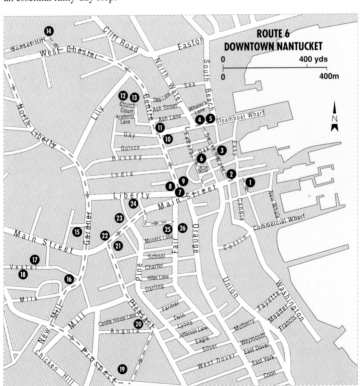

**ROUTE 6
DOWNTOWN NANTUCKET**

Whaling Museum

Pacific National Bank

Continuing on South Water, walk up a block to visit the ★★★ **Whaling Museum** (tel: 228-1736) ❹. Built as a spermaceti candle factory following the 1846 fire, the museum has several essential exhibits including its 46-foot (14-meter) finback whale skeleton, nautical paintings, and the tools of the trade – harpoon, lance and whaleboat. A replica of a ship's onboard 'tryworks' displays how whale blubber was boiled into oil, alongside the more unexpected byproducts of long sea journeys – handcarved scrimshaw and woven 'lightship baskets' which have become closely identified with the island. The museum offers guided tours, lectures and a gift shop of Nantucket crafts.

Next door, the ★ **Peter Folger Research Center** ❺ offers a varying selection of island artifacts, paintings and furniture. Folger was an early settler who helped negotiate with the Wampanoags for land in the 17th century. He was also Benjamin Franklin's grandfather and a relative of island-born coffee mogul James Folger. The second floor contains archives of island lore, available to researchers through the island's Historical Society.

Turn left onto Federal Street and follow it to the intersection with Lower Indian Street. The Greek Revival structure at the corner is the ★★★ **Nantucket Atheneum** ❻, with its unmistakable fluted Ionic columns. The Atheneum was built by popular island architect Frederick Coleman six months after the original burned in the fire of 1846. Maria Mitchell, the astronomer, was the Atheneum's first librarian at the age of 18, and she brought such luminaries as Frederick Douglass and Henry David Thoreau to the Atheneum's Great Hall, where history's thorniest issues were duly thrashed out. The hall and its adjoining garden still host lectures and performances, while the library contains rare 19th century volumes, portraits and one-of-a-kind manuscripts. The public library here contains the town's 40,000 book holdings.

Back at the head of Main Street Square is the ★ **Pacific National Bank** (tel: 228-1917) ❼, built in 1818 of imported pressed brick. The Bank has had something of a charmed life: not only did it survive the 1846 fire and the Great Depression, but on its roof Maria Mitchell discovered her famous comet in the fall of 1847. The streets of downtown are still so gently lit that you can see the stars from Main Street.

Next door is the Doric-pillared **United Methodist Church** ❽. Constructed in 1823 as Methodism had begun to supplant Quaker beliefs on the island, the church is still active and houses the Actor's Theatre of Nantucket (tel: 223-6325) in its basement, as well as the Island Stage (tel: 228-6620) and photographer Cary Hazlegrove's slide-introduction to the island (tel: 228-3783).

Across the square from the church is an island institution: **Murray's Toggery Shop** (tel: 228-0437, 800-368-2134) **9**, where shoppers can purchase 'Nantucket Reds': cotton shorts, skirts and pants designed to fade into a preppy rose. Murray's, which also has a bargain outlet on New Street and two more shops on the Vineyard, stocks practical sweaters, gloves and scarves well into the spring for unexpected squalls. Murray's was also the site of the first Macy's shop, where Rowland Macy worked before following the Gold Rush west in 1849 and finally returning to New York to open R.H. Macy & Company.

Nantucket Red cap

Follow Centre Street north again to Broad Street and the **★★ Jared Coffin House** (tel: 228-2405, 800-248-2405) **10**. Shipping merchant Coffin built this three-story brick house, the largest in town, in 1845, when his socialite wife decided that their original address at Moor's End was too far out of town. After only two years in town, the Coffins migrated to Boston, and the house has since evolved into one of the island's most popular inns. Current innkeeper Phil Read, who purchased the building in 1976 from the Historical Trust, furnished the lobby with antiques to match the inn's lavishly pillared doorway. Included in the inn's five surrounding houses is the Greek Revival **Harrison Gray House**. A full Greek Revival, built in 1841 for the captain of the whaling ship *Nantucket.*

Jared Coffin House

49

Across the street from the Coffin House, the Seven Seas Gift Shop marks the former home of Captain George Pollard. Herman Melville based at least part of *Moby Dick* on Pollard's ship, the *Essex,* which was rammed and sunk by a whale in 1820 with Pollard's nephew on-board as cabin boy. Stranded at sea, Pollard and the others survived by cannibalism, and his nephew was first to go.

The Coffin House establishes the unofficial northern counterpart to Main Street Square, At the same intersection is the subterranean **Brotherhood of Thieves 11**, one of the island's better-kept secrets. Named after an 1844 Nantucket pamphlet titled 'The Brotherhood of Thieves: or a True Picture of the American Church and Clergy,' this old whaling bar doesn't take credit cards and has no listed telephone number. But it has excellent pub food and chowder, and a casual candle-lit ambience.

Singing in the sun

Continue up Centre Street to the corner of Step Lane and the **★ First Congregational Church** (tel: 228-0950) **12**. Built in 1834 by Boston's Samuel Waldon, the Gothic Revival church has a 120-foot (37-meter) tower offering a dazzling view of the town and island. The original steeple was built in 1848 but replaced in 1968 because of its vulnerability to Nantucket's high winds and nor'easters. Down below, E.H. Whitaker's *trompe l'oeil* artistry and a massive, 600-pound brass chandelier are almost as impressive as the view up above. The 1725 vestry behind the church makes it the island's oldest house of worship. Next door to the church, the **Anchor Inn** (tel: 228-0072) **⑬**, built in 1806, offers 11 rooms of in-town sanctuary in the former home of harpooner Archaelus Hammond. He was the first captain to harpoon a whale in the Pacific.

Jethro Coffin house, interior

Follow the curve of Centre Street to Sunset Hill Road and the ★★★ **Jethro Coffin House** (tel: 228-1894) **⑭**. Commonly thought to be the island's oldest house, this National Landmark saltbox dates to 1686, when it was built as a wedding gift for Jethro Coffin and Mary Gardner by their land-feuding fathers, two of the island's first settlers. With this house, whose chimney horseshoe design is sometimes hypothesized to represent the union of two families, the Gardners and Coffins ended the argument between full-share and part-share factions. The house itself was nearly destroyed by lightning in 1987, but restoration work by the Historical Association makes it a must-see exhibit.

Fire hose cart

From Sunset Hill, follow North Liberty Street to the left until it becomes Gardner Street. At the intersection of Howard Street is the ★ **Old Fire Hose Cart House** (tel: 228-1893) **⑮**, of particular interest because of the conflagration which destroyed so much of downtown. The station, built in 1886, is the last of its kind on the island. On display is the 19th-century fire pumper *Siasconset*. Behind the Cart House is **Greater Light**, a converted barn where the Historical Association exhibits decorative art from the Early American period and the Far East.

Whale Skeleton, Maria Mitchell
Science Center

Follow Gardner to Vestal Street and the ★★★ **Maria Mitchell Science Center** (tel: 228-9198) **⑯**. From her birth on the island in 1818, Maria (pronounced *Ma-rye-ah*) proved to be of exceptional genius, charting eclipses with her father, setting navigation instruments for local sailors and by age 18, running the Nantucket Atheneum. She was awarded a gold medal from the King of Denmark for her discovery of a comet. Although she had no formal higher education beyond the Nantucket schools, she became the first female astronomy professor in the country, teaching at Vassar until her death in 1889. In 1902, three of Mitchell's cousins founded a non-profit organization to encourage scientific exploration on the island, particularly among children. Most of the Mitchell Association's facilities are open to the public – a science library, a natural history museum, the Mitchell Birthplace and the Loines Observatory on the Milk Street Extension.

Further down Vestal Street on the right is the island's ★ **Old Gaol** (tel: 228-1894) **⑰**. Built in 1805, this unassuming, shingled facade covers an iron-and-oak bolted

Old Gaol security

51

strongbox whose four barred cells held its criminals until 1933. Two of the cells have fireplaces, and the 'violent ward' is a room sheathed on the inside with lead. There are pit toilets and plank bunks, although most of Nantucket's prisoners were allowed to go home at night, having no real chance of escape. The Historical Society keeps this free exhibit open for visitors to explore on their own.

Across from the Gaol is the last remaining **cooperage** ⓲ on the island, where whale oil casks were made from tupelo, or beetlebung, trees. In the mid-1800s the island's cooperages were an entire industry in themselves, rising and falling with the fortunes of whaling. Today the structure is a private residence.

The Old Mill

From Vestal Street, turn left on Prospect Street and follow it down to the Old Mill Park. The ★ **Old Mill** itself (tel: 228-1894) ⓳ was built from shipwreck wood by sailor Nathan Wilbur in 1746, making it perhaps the oldest in the country – a fact even more impressive since it's been in continuous use since then. The arms are 30 feet long and 6 feet wide, covered in sail-cloth, and inside the original one-ton stoneworks grind corn for bread. Visitors have the opportunity to buy bread after watching it being made.

Walk north on South Mill Street. Just before Pleasant Avenue, the road passes the 1834 **Moor's End** ⓴, a privately owned Georgian brick mansion where Jared Coffin and his wife lived before they moved up to Broad Street. Known in part by its distinctive brick-walled garden, Moor's End was the first major brick house on the island, setting a pattern for scores of others. Inside the dining room murals depict whaling voyages like the ones that made Coffin's fortune.

Turn left onto Pleasant Avenue, following it back to Main Street. Here the ★★ **Hadwen Houses** (tel: 228-1894) ㉑ were built for the Starbuck sisters right across the street

The Three Bricks

from where their brothers lived. In 1845, whaling mogul Joseph Starbuck hired island architect Frederick Brown Coleman to build these two Greek Revival Houses for his daughters, one of whom married merchant William Hadwen, whose factory is now the Whaling Museum. The Historical Association owns the houses now, and has restored their interior to mid-19th century grandeur.

By 1840, Starbuck had already hired builders to produce three identical Georgian mansions for his three sons, William, George and Matthew, facing his daughters' houses but architecturally worlds apart from them.★★ **The Three Bricks** ㉒ were built by Cape Cod carpenters and masons for between $40,000 and $50,000. Starbuck prudently held onto the title until the sons became full partners in the business. He owned 23 whaleships, including the *Three Brothers,* which set out in 1854 on a record-breaking five-year voyage and returned with an unprecedented 6,000 barrels of whale oil.

Continue on Main Street to Winter Street and turn left to the ★ **Isaac Coffin School** (tel: 228-2505) ㉓. British Loyalist Coffin had this Greek Revival structure assembled in 1852 for descendants of the Coffin family (about half the island's population). Prior to its construction, island children could only attend 'cent schools' where parents sent them off with a penny a day to pay for lessons. The structure now is home for the Nantucket Chamber Music Center, as well as an island school resource center.

Easy rider

Returning to Main, turn right on Walnut Street. At the corner of Walnut and Liberty is the ★★ **Macy-Christian House** (tel: 228-1894)㉔. Built in 1740 by island merchant Thomas Macy, the house served Macy's family for 87 years. In 1934 Reverend George Christian and his wife moved in, refurbishing the interior, and tour guides explain the different periods of renovation. Colonial Revival antiques and artifacts decorate the interior, some of them quite beautiful.

Quaker Meeting House

Take Walnut back across Main Street. Turn right on Rays Court and right again on Fair Street. To your left is the ★ **Quaker Meeting House** (tel: 228-0136) ㉕. Inside this deliberately plain, rectangular house, Friends' meetings still occur on Sundays throughout the summer, and visitors are always welcome to sit in with this group, whose philosophical and religious tenets were powerfully influential on the island for two centuries.

Next to the Meeting House, the ★★ **Fair Street Museum** (tel: 228-0722) ㉖ displays paintings by local members of the Nantucket Artists Association. John Singleton Copley, Childe Hassam and others visited and painted on the island, and their work hangs here along with that of contemporary artists.

Route 7

Points East

Seaside fun

Outside of town, the island's 10,000 acres (4,000 hectares) of moors give way to a shoreline that is almost entirely beach – some of the best on the east coast. Nantucket's eastern and southern shores host small communities and settlements and occasional gray-shingled houses have sprouted up among the low, rolling hills. Almost a third of the island is now protected from further development. Rent a car or a moped (cycling can be exhausting unless you're used to miles of legwork) and sample the unspoiled environment of an ecosystem purified by the sea.

Begin the tour at Surfside Beach, on the island's south shore. Here, besides the usual swimming and windsurfing, is the ★ **Robert B. Johnson AYH-Hostel** (tel: 228-0433), the most scenically located youth hostel in New England. Built in an 1874 lifesaving station, the hostel offers refuge to weary cyclists and backpackers. It has a 10.30pm curfew and the island's most reasonable rates.

Cranberries for conservation

Take Surfside Road north and turn right onto Fairground Road. Bear left on Old South Road, which connects to Milestone Road or 'Sconset Road (Nantucketers long ago abbreviated Siasconset, just as Vineyarders made short work of Chappaquiddick). Milestone leads east past the Nantucket Conservation Foundation's ★ **Cranberry Bog**. In the mid-19th century, cranberries became a cash crop here. October is the 'wet harvest,' when the bogs are flooded and 'beaters' remove the cranberries from their vines. They float, forming huge shoals of red, and are scooped and loaded for the Ocean Spray Company as well as local honeys and preserves. The profits help the Conservation Foundation's efforts to preserve the island's land.

Sconset values its privacy

Chanticleer Inn

Sankaty Lighthouse

Follow Milestone Road out to the far eastern shore and the village of ★★★ **Sconset ❶**. Deriving its name from the Wampanoag *missiaskonsatt,* meaning 'near the great whale-bone,' the village is built along the white sand cliffs of Sankaty Head, the first recorded landmark made by navigator George Waymouth in 1604. Sconset was settled in the 17th century for whalers and fishermen and later became the first resort area on the island. Whaleships were still voyaging out – and the Sankaty Lighthouse not yet constructed – when the Atlantic Hotel was built here in 1842. In 1884 the Nantucket Railroad extended its rails from Surfside to Sconset, and continued in different incarnations (including the gasoline-powered *Bug and the Bird Cage*, which once completed its 19-minute run from town by flying right off the tracks) until 1917.

Walk down Broadway to view the village's first 17th and 18th-century cottages. They were originally dirt-floored, without windows or kitchens, built to house six-man whale-boat crews before they shipped out of Sconset. Gradually the fishermen's wives and families moved in, adding 'warts' – additional rooms – and more homey amenities, resulting in these dollhouse-like cottages.

A prime example of this fish-shack architecture is **Auld Lang Syne**, once a makeshift post-office for Nantucketer William Baxter. When the US Post Office found out that Baxter had hung out a shingle reading 'Post Office' and was charging Sconset residents a penny per letter to carry their mail to town every day on his wagon, they sent an investigator to the island. Baxter himself picked the man up in town, drove him 10 miles (16km) north of Sconset and sent him back home, satisfied that the rumors were false. Several years later the house – which still sits on Broadway among other historic cottages – was officially recognized as Sconset's legitimate Post Office.

Just up New Street, between West Chapel Street and Park Lane, is the celebrated **Chanticleer Inn** (tel: 257-6231). The Inn's French cuisine and rose-covered courtyard regularly place it among the top 50 restaurants in the world, with a wine cellar that is often ranked among the top 10. Chef Jean-Charles Berruet's specialties make use of local seafood and fowl, though preparation and presentation create the real magic of a $60 prix fixe menu. Reservations and a dinner jacket are musts, but take-out is available at the Beach Street outlet (tel: 325-5625).

From the 1776 water pump at the center of the village, take a left on Sankaty Avenue and continue for about a mile to the ★★ **Sankaty Lighthouse**. Built in 1851, it was fitted with one of the original state-of-the-art Fresnel lenses and is the second most powerful beacon in the area, second only to the Cape Cod or Highland Light in Truro. It is visible for 24 miles (40km) out to sea.

Follow Sankaty Avenue until it becomes Polpis Road heading north. Jog left briefly on Quidnet Road, then turn right on Wauwinet Road. Continuing north, you'll find yourself situated between the harbor and the ocean, on a narrow strip of sand that fisherman called a 'haulover,' because they would drag their boats across to avoid detouring around **Great Point.**

Beginning here is a 1,100-acre (445-hectare) wildlife sanctuary, the ★★ **Coskata-Coatue Wildlife Refuge** (tel: 228-6799). The Nantucket Trustees of the Reservations offer a popular 3-hour over-sand tour that leaves from the Wauwinet Inn parking lot. Visitors may see everything from snowy egrets to the tiny, running sanderlings which fly to the Arctic every year to nest.

Touring in style

The ★★ **Great Point Lighthouse**, first glimpsed on the ferry ride into the harbor, sits at the tip of the point. From the first wooden tower in 1784, the original rubblestone lighthouse was built in 1816 and smashed by a spring Nor'easter in 1984. What stands in its place is a replica, constructed two years later by the Boston engineering firm Ganteaume & McMullen and partially powered by solar panels. This time Nantucketers took no chances: the tower's cofferdam foundation is buried more than 30 feet (9 meter) into the beach, supporting its 5-foot-thick cement mat. Should Great Point itself wash away, the structure can serve as an off-shore light, with an anticipated 100 year life-cycle.

55

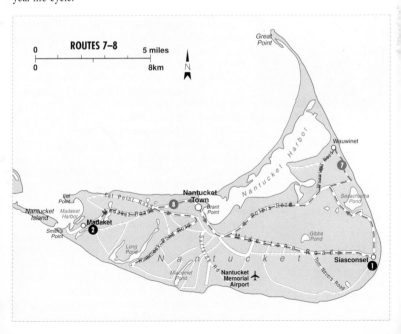

From Wauwinet Road, retrace your steps down to Polpis Road again and turn right, back toward town. ★ **Polpis Harbor** is accessible by a rough dirt road road to your left. What was the island's busiest farmland a century ago is now either privately owned or put into conservation. At the far end of the harbor is the private Bayberry Farm, built in 1965 by Nantucket Historical Association Museum Shop creator Grace Grossman and her husband Bernard, using wood from an old farmhouse.

Continue along Polpis Road until you reach a short unpaved trail on the left leading to ★★ **Altar Rock**, 90 feet (27 meters) above sea level and the highest point on the island. The rock offers a 360° panorama.

Across from Altar Rock is ★ **Quaise**, which backs up to an inlet on Nantucket Harbor. It was here, during the Revolution, that island Tory and staunch Loyalist Kezia Coffin forged a lucrative smuggler's trade with the British ships blockading the harbor. Kezia and her husband John Coffin routinely sent sloops through the blockade at night, and charged exorbitant prices for the goods they brought onto the island, until the Quakers 'read her out of the meeting' and other islanders joined together to bankrupt the Coffin holdings after the war. Now the area belongs to newer, private houses, and the secret tunnel where Kezia supposedly stored her smuggled goods was never located.

Polpis Road follows the curve of the harbor past communities of summer houses and the **University of Massachusetts Field Station**. This is one of the island's two institutions offering college credit year-round, the other being the School of Design and the Arts on Wauwinet Road. The field station mixes the natural sciences with humanities, and students are mixed between off-islanders and Nantucket residents. Although there are no tours, visits to the field house may be arranged by appointment.

Life Saving Museum

Continuing on Polpis Road, head toward town until you reach the ★ **Life Saving Museum**. First constructed at Surfside in 1874, this structure was originally known as a 'humane' house and the rescue teams were called humane societies. Inside are 18th century lifesaving boats, buoys and other artifacts used during shipwreck rescues. The museum now faces out of Polpis Harbor to the north.

To the right, Monomoy Road leads out to some of the oldest summer homes on the island, many of them built during World War I. ★ **Monomoy** offers its own unique view of the harbor. Like Polpis, Monomoy was farmland before it became prime real estate. Its creeks and shorelines are rich with sought-after Nantucket Bay scallops. Canadian geese and swans skim along the water between here and the Brant Point light across the harbor.

From Monomoy, return to town via Orange Street, which connects to Polpis Road, and conclude the tour.

Route 8

The smartest transportation

Points West *See map on page 55*

West of town, Nantucket becomes an island for natural-
ists, hikers and cyclists. Although Sherburne, the island's
first white settlement, was established here in the 'cradle' between Capaum Pond and Hummock Farm in 1660,
history has left little observable trace of itself here. In 1700,
a savage Nor'easter expanded a sandbar at the mouth of
Sherburne's harbor, sealing it off and turning it into a pond.
No longer able to fish or sail schooners from their current location, Sherburne moved *en masse* to the present
location of town, changing its name to Nantucket in 1795.

57

Sand, sea and serenity

   The unofficial center of Sherburne was Parliament
House, the home of Nathaniel and Mary Starbuck. Married in 1662 and the first white couple to have a child on
Nantucket, the Starbucks made their home at Parliament
House for 60 years. Parliament House now stands reassembled on Pine Street in town, its northern part mostly
unchanged from its original design. Almost all the other
houses of the intial Sherburne settlement were demolished
for wood, always a scarcity on the island.

   Only one trace of the original settlement remains, the
1722 Elihu Coleman House, secreted away off Madaket
Road. Although the privately-owned house is inaccessi-
ble to visitors, Coleman himself deserves mention as one
of the country's first abolitionists, and it was here that
he composed a largely overlooked *Testimony Against That
Anti Christian Practice of Making Slaves of Men*. A century later, when New England and particularly the Quakers of Nantucket were speaking out fiercely against
slavery, Coleman's treatise was honored by William Lloyd
Garrison, who made a pilgrimage out to the house itself.

   For maps and wildlife information at the beginning of
this route, stop about a mile west of town on Cliff Road
at the Nantucket Conservation Foundation.

*Brant Point lighthouse
and life guard station*

Capaum Pond

Start at the harbor and travel north on South Beach Street to Harbor View Way to the ★ **Children's Beach**, next to the Steamship Wharf. The beach has playground equipment, a food stand, lifeguards and a gentle surf.

Continuing north on South Beach, turn right on Easton Street and follow it out to the ★★ **Brant Point Lighthouse**. The original 1746 lighthouse was the first of its kind in the Cape area, replacing such lesser signals as a lantern hung between two poles or larger lanterns mounted on wooden platforms. The red beacon is an occulting light, meaning that it is darkened at regular intervals – in this case, every four seconds. The undertow makes swimming risky here, but Brant Point itself presents an ideal vista to observe harbor traffic, sunbathe or have a picnic.

Turn back and follow Easton Street westward until it becomes Cliff Road. On your right is Macy's Pond, and just before it, a dirt road heads out to the Founding Father's Burying Ground. Travel for 3 miles (5km) to Madaket Road, joining Cliff Road from the left. The dirt road leading off to the right takes you to ★ **Capaum Pond** near where Thomas Macy's first settlers created Sherburne. Initially Macy had come with his wife, five children, Edward Starbuck and 12-year-old Isaac Coleman, but the following spring and summer their numbers swelled to 60.

The settlers built a gristmill on the pond, and although the soil was not rich, managed to farm corn, oats and rye. In accordance with Thomas Mayhew's rulings for fair treatment of the natives, the settlers reimbursed them in kind for the land they farmed. Too late, the Wampanoags realized they had forfeited their livelihood, their land and future. Diseases of the white settlers, and their 'firewater,' exacted a crushing blow on the indigenous population. Unlike Martha's Vineyard, Nantucket now has no existing Indian population now: the last native died in 1854.

Continue along Madaket Road and turn right on Eel Point Road to ★★ **Dionis Beach**, named after the wife of settler Tristam Coffin. The Coffins helped populate the island with nine children and 74 grandchildren, resulting less than 25 years later in over 1,582 descendants. The beach is occupied in the summer months by swimmers and in the winter by gulls, shellfish and horseshoe crab. There are life guards and restrooms here, and the surf is gentle for swimming.

Dionis beach

Return to Madaket Road and continue onward to ★★★ **Madaket ❷**, which is the island's westernmost harbor and was the original landfall for the first white settlers. Offering the perfect sunset, Madaket overlooks Tuckernuck and Esther Island, originally called Old Smith Point until Hurricane Esther cut it off from the rest of the island in 1971. The shifting sands have since reattached Esther to Madaket – a vivid illustration of Nantucket's protean landscape.

Grey seals swim up ★ **Hither Creek** in pursuit of herring, and lounge conspicuously in the harbor alongside waterbirds such as the snowy owl, egret and tern. Shellfishing and scalloping is very popular, although the November to March harvesting season can make it chilly. To the north of Madaket Beach is Eel Point, owned by the Nantucket Conservation Foundation. The Maria Mitchell Association's Natural Science Department (tel: 228-0898) hosts a variety of nature walks for hikers and birdwatchers here, including a self-guided tour which leads to Eel Point.

Return to town on Madaket Road. Take a right onto Winn Street, and another right on the Milk Street Extension. You'll pass the Maria Mitchell Association's ★★ **Loines Observatory** (tel: 228-9273). The observatory is open to the public on clear Wednesday evenings during the summer and hosts lectures on Monday nights. Seminars are held with visiting scientists and educators, and much of the material is geared toward children, in tune with the Association's commitment to encouraging scientific exploration by young people.

Continue on Milk Street until you reach Hummock Pond Road. In the summer months you'll pass farm stands offering fresh produce, and signs for nearby Bartlett Farm, as well as Serenity Farm, Surfside and Mt. Vernon Farm, whose stables offer boarding facilities and jump courses. Follow this road down to ★★ **Cisco Beach**. Swimmers and surfers flock here in August, and there is a lifeguard on duty but no other facilities on the beach itself. There are summer cottages for rent between Cisco and Hummock Pond for those who don't mind the 4-mile (6-km) 'commute' into town.

Cisco beach

Artistic Heritage

Architecture

Opposite: Gothic cottage in Oak Bluffs

Housing styles on both the Vineyard and Nantucket have always flourished and sputtered with the changing times, illustrating the islands' ups and downs more vividly than any timeline. When the money was plentiful, builders and architects spared no expense. But in the beginning Yankee ingenuity concentrated first and foremost on bare-bones practicality. Perseverence was necessary: fires, wars and economic crises provided both islands with setbacks serious enough to force them to begin all over again.

Ecclesiastical influence

On the Vineyard and Nantucket, the rudimentary Cape Cod designs combined the luxury of increased craftsmanship with the echoes of Devon and Cornwall. One-room structures with wattle-and-daub insulation and a massive central chimney, these square buildings had a main door with one window on either side – a 'half-Cape' – which later expanded with the family fortune into full two-door Cape, with a master bedroom and a parlor. By the early 1700s, architects had expanded the Cape upward, into the saltbox-design adopted from Kent, and outward into a rear ell, or lean-to, for the kitchen in back. The development of the mansard or gambrel roof created extra upstairs space for additional family members.

61

The New England Colonial style began as a necessary modification of 18th-century Georgian England, the era before the whaling boom truly began. Rather than building mansions of stone and brick, islanders used wood (often carving or painting it to resemble brick), creating wide central halls with additional fireplaces and enlarged staircases. Older houses simply refurbished their original doorways with pilasters, pediments and elliptical cranberry-glass fanlights and sidelights. Genuine examples of brick Georgian mansions – most notably Joseph Starbuck's Three Bricks – appeared at the tail-end of the era, when whaling merchants could finally afford it.

Wood was the main material

The confidence of America's builders reached new heights with the Federal period (1776–1830), when the islands' architectures no longer seemed to be competing self-consciously with British style but – with its newly enlarged windowpanes, open spiral staircases and elegantly balustraded widows' walks – looking forward confidently to its own future.

By 1840, the elegance and restraint of the Federal style blended into the popularity of Jeffersonian Greek Revival, sometimes in the same structure, as in the Vineyard's Daniel Fisher House. As men like Fisher, and Nantucket's Starbuck and Jared Coffin amassed huge whaling fortunes, the architectural floodgates burst with dazzling amalgams of Federal, Empire and Greek Revival, as exhibited by

Daniel Fisher House

William Hadwen's 'Two Greeks' on Nantucket's Main Street.

The Carpenter Gothic style

In the mid to late 19th century, Victorian pretense collided with the invention of the jigsaw to produce the Vineyard's Carpenter Gothic style, displayed with such flash and filigree in the Oak Bluffs campground. Late 19th-century upper-class modifications on this wedding-cake ornamentation led to the Queen Anne houses of Ocean Park, with their unmistakable spires and fish-scale roofs. Equally distinctive are the islands' gray-shingle houses, marking the first insurgence of summer visitors between 1880 and 1920, and their working-class counterpart, the gray fishermans' cottages of Menemsha's fishing village. America's postwar housing boom, peaking in the '80s, brought its share of rather bland ranch houses to the Cape and islands, but – aesthetically welcome or not – they too provide an historical footnote: the migration of the middle-class toward a seasonal leisure-class, and toward the relative seclusion of the islands.

Art and literature

Nantucket Island found its literary bards early on, in the form of Melville, Thoreau, Emerson and Nathaniel Hawthorne, who composed much of his *Twice Told Tales* on the island. The novelists and playwrights who have flocked to the islands since have used them more as a window on the world than a setting in itself, but world literature has reaped the benefit.

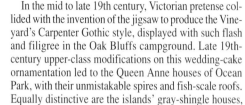

Pulitzer Prize-winner Thornton Wilder wrote his final novel here, after a career which included *The Bridge of San Luis Rey* and *Our Town*. Lillian Hellman and Dashiell Hammet bought a house in Vineyard Haven in the 1950s, and often went bluefishing with neighbor John Hersey. Vineyarder Katherine Chirgwin, who along with her husband owned Edgartown's Colonial Inn, remembers typing Somerset Maugham's manuscript for *The Razor's Edge* when Maugham was summering at the inn in 1943. 'He didn't cross his t's or dot his i's,' she recalls, 'so it took me quite a while to catch on.'

Somerset Maugham

All the news

Currently, Pulitzer-winners William Styron and David McCullough make summer and year-round homes here respectively (the Vineyard may have more Pulitzers per square foot than anywhere besides Manhattan), along with journalists Art Buchwald and Richard Reston (son of *New York Times* columnist James 'Scotty' Reston, who bought the *Vineyard Gazette* from Henry Beetle Hough). Columnist and author Russell Baker has long summered on Nantucket. Novelist Ward Just and his wife live on the Vineyard's Lambert's Cove, and longtime Oak Bluffs resident Dorothy West of the Harlem Renaissance set her highly-acclaimed novel *The Wedding* here. In fact, the continuing flow of literary traffic is such that references to the Vineyard settings invariably pop up in bestsellers by Richard North Patterson and Alice Hoffman, whose novel *Illumination Night* is proudly displayed with other island books at Vineyard Haven's Bunch of Grapes Bookstore. Each summer the bookstore hosts a series of public readings by such varied talent as Mary Higgins Clark, Erica Jong, Robert Parker (of the Spencer mysteries) and Alan Dershowitz.

Artists throughout the century have come to both islands to paint, sketch and photograph the landscape. Alfred Eisenstaedt, Thomas Hart Benton and Jackson Pollack – along with Jules Feiffer and Shel Silverstein – have all kept cottages and studios on the Vineyard. Nantucket's exemplary museums and galleries, including the Fair Street Museum and the Gallery at Four India Street, display work by Americans Rembrandt Peale, John Singleton Copley, and Childe Hassam.

During the summer tour of Nantucket's private houses in August, visitors may catch a glimpse of the *trompe l'oeil* and mural work of Stanley J. Rowland – whose 1926 whaling mural adorns the living room of Moor's End – and local painter Gail Sharrets. The work of contemporary artists and photographers such as landscapist John Osborne and William Welch insure that the tradition of excellence will continue into the future.

63

Nantucket has long attracted designers and craftspeople from more metropolitan areas, including London's Erica Wilson, whose Main Street Needle Works provides a more relaxed counterpart to her Madison Avenue boutique as well as providing detailed textile replicas for the Historical Association's Jared Coffin House. From Stephen Swift's handmade furniture to Claire Murray's hooked rugs, Nantucket overflows with a wealth of artfully-wrought treasures.

The Vineyard hosts its own long-standing line-up of craftspeople, from metal sculptor and weather vane builder Travis Tuck to the rug-hooking of the McAdoo family, whose work is displayed at the Granary Gallery. Printmaker Michele Ratte, whose hand-dyed and silk-screened fabrics have such universal appeal that Hollywood costume designers have begun to use them onscreen, works year-round out of West Tisbury. Chilmark wool becomes expertly woven blankets and sweaters at Clarissa Allen's 300-year-old family farm, while Vineyard Haven's Valerie Beggs offers her own wool waders through Vineyard Haven's upscale LeRoux.

Granary Gallery

Like Nantucket, the Vineyard remains a community – too rare in the age of mass-production – where mastery and commitment to craft are recognized and rewarded by both summer visitors and islanders.

Festivals

Spring fever in Nantucket

Escaping the crowds

Every month there's a celebration on the islands – even January has a chili-tasting contest – but May through September encompass the most colorful happenings. Nantucket's colors come out slightly earlier than the Vineyard's, in the last weekend of April, with the very successful Daffodil Festival Weekend. Begun in 1974 by Jean MacAusland, the wife of the publisher of *Gourmet* magazine, this Nantucket Garden Club celebration infuses the island's main streets with over a million daffodils. Antique cars parade out to Sconset for a picnic, all decorated with the bright yellow flowers, and the American Daffodil Society judges floral arrangements and displays in town. In May, Nantucketers and New Englanders take to the water with the island's annual 200-vessel Figawi Race from Hyannis to the island, the first major boat race of the year.

Both islands celebrate Memorial Day as the unofficial beginning of 'the season.' Nantucket launches its annual Bluefish Tournament, while the Vineyard holds its traditional ceremony with island children throwing bouquets from Edgartown's Memorial Dock to commemorate islanders lost at sea. The Vineyard Playhouse, with its annual short-play festival, begins its professional summer season. Book early – several months is not overcautious – if you intend to bring your car over or find a hotel room for this long weekend.

In mid-June, Nantucket hosts the Cranberry Classic, one of the season's traditional foot races. The last weekend in June spotlights the Harborfest celebration: a windsurfing regatta, activities and parades at Children's Beach, and the Nantucket Yacht Club's Gifford Bowl occur during this weekend as well. Independence Day marks another high-point for weekend activity. Both islands vie for the most elaborate fireworks display: Nantucket's, on Jetties Beach, the Vineyard's in Edgartown.

July on the Vineyard is the month of the Edgartown Yacht Club's Regatta, the largest and most prestigious in the area. The town of Tisbury celebrates its birthday by closing off Main Street for its annual street fair, and the month wraps up with the Portuguese community's Feast of the Holy Ghost in Oak Bluffs. Some of the most ornate whaling houses in Edgartown are also opened in the annual Harbor House Tour during the last week of July.

August is, quite simply, *the* month to come to the islands – or stay away, depending on your feelings about crowds. They will be everywhere, and unavoidable. The Nantucket Garden Club holds its annual tour of private homes this month, with different houses featured each year. The Vineyard offers its increasingly famous Possible Dreams Auction to benefit Martha's Vineyard Community Services, with auctioneer Art Buchwald at the gavel. In the past, auction participants have bid on such prizes as a tour of CBS Studios with Mike Wallace, a personal performance from Carly Simon, or an afternoon sail with Walter Cronkite. The auction is held by the pool at the Harborview Resort in Edgartown.

Also in August is Oak Bluffs' annual Illumination Night, when the gingerbread cottages, trees, fences and posts in the Methodist campground are strung with thousands of Japanese lanterns. Begun in 1879 to mark the closing of the camp ground for another season, this traditional has since become hugely popular, and as a result the exact date is kept secret until the last minute. The West Tisbury Agricultural Fair is another long-running August attraction, dating back more than 130 years, with everything from livestock competitions to carnival rides and music at the Fairgrounds.

In September, Nantucket usually holds its County Fair, while the Vineyard schedules Tivoli Day, a tradition which dates to the 1870s, when Tivoli was the name of an Oak Bluffs' skating rink and dance hall, as well as the popular song 'Tivoli Girl.' Bicyclists race around the island, as well as competing in shorter competitions. The Vineyard's Striped Bass & Bluefish Derby begins this month too, and fishermen from all over New England and beyond compete for prizes throughout September and into October.

Raking in the bounty

October marks Nantucket's Cranberry Harvest. The Windswept Cranberry Bog offers tours, cranberry cooking contests and crafts, as the bogs are flooded and the berries plucked, raked and loaded into trucks. The Columbus Day Road Race from Sconset into town marks the unofficial end of the season here, as does its Vineyard counterpart, the Oak Bluffs 5K Road Race.

Just when the pulse of the islands seem to have lulled, November heralds the holiday season. Nantucket Noel traditionally involves the planting of live Christmas trees all up and down Main Street from the Pacific Bank to the waterfront, where island children decorate them with everything from painted scallop shells and strung cranberries to miniature Nantucket light baskets.

Young revellers

On the Vineyard, Christmas has to be split between Vineyard Haven's 'Twelve Days of Christmas' activities, and Edgartown's more traditional Old Fashioned Christmas Celebration. For years the island Minnesingers have held their annual Holiday Concert at the Old Whaling Church in Edgartown. There are horse-and-buggy rides, walking tours and the arrival of Santa at the Edgartown Christmas tree. On New Year's Eve, the island's Crossover Ball has recently become the most talked-about new tradition, where cross-dressing is not only encouraged but judged and awarded prizes at the Playhouse.

Food and Drink

Visitors come to the islands expecting excellent seafood and get it. Fresh bluefish, striped bass, swordfish, cod, clams and bay scallops, jumbo shrimp and, of course, lobster, are only part of the day's haul.

But island cuisine is only partly about seafood. Local farms provide fresh produce and dairy goods, fruits, sauces and chutneys. In summer, both islands supply restaurants with just-picked vegetables and locally-grown herbs, and adventurous visitors may wish to forage local farm stands themselves to assemble a home-cooked feast. (On the Vineyard, check out Pesto Vineyardo at the West Tisbury Farmers' Market for that extra Parmesan zing.)

Dining out can add up quickly, particularly if you like to sit down and be waited on for every meal. The price-gap has widened between ambient dining and cheap take-out, crowding out much mid-priced family fare. Feeding a group of four at many of the 'corner luncheonettes' or cafes might find you forking out over $80 for lunch, drinks, dessert and a tip (ubiquitous 'tip-jars' sit on every take-out counter, but you shouldn't feel obligated unless you've been seated and waited on). Best, perhaps, to grab a lobster roll or a bowl of chowder for noon and make reservations to splurge on a harborfront dinner. Be aware that, with waterfront dining, the view is built right into the price.

That said, atmosphere and appetite *can* both be appeased without emptying your wallet. Both islands abound with outdoor ambience that turn magical at sunset, and some of the most acclaimed eateries offer take-out – grab something to go at the Home Port in Menemsha, a half-pound of boiled prawn and cocktail sauce at Vineyard Haven's Net Result, or carry out world-class cuisine from the Chanticleer outlet on Beach Street in Nantucket. If you don't mind picnic tables and beach blankets, there's a new world of freshly-shucked oysters and jumbo servings of shrimp at seafood outlets like Poole's Fish and the Menemsha Bite. Of course, these being 'the islands,' casual dining and lack of pretension will be the order of the day even inside the priciest of restaurants – only Chanticleer requires a jacket, and you'll rarely spot a tie.

Fruits and Bakeries, Sugar and Spice
Both islands abound with local produce, from the Vineyard's pick-your-own at Thimble Farm (tel: 693-6396) to the Bartlett Farm's fruit and vegetable carts in Main Street Square. Because autumn is so mild on Nantucket, the island's farms offer produce that cannot grow on the Vineyard and the Cape. Nantucket's cranberry bog is one of the country's largest, and in the October harvest season, cooking contests are usually part of the festivities. Freshly-

Opposite: the local wine

Ice-cream sauces

Pick-your-own lobster

Chanticleer service

Dried cranberries

canned cranberry preserves and relishes are available at shops in town – even a zesty cranberry barbecue sauce for the bold – as are fresh breads and rolls to spread them on, at the Downy Flake on Children's Beach (tel: 228-4533). On the Vineyard, Chicama Vineyards produces 8,000 cases of locally-pressed wine a year (see below for the inconvenient news about drink on the Vineyard) as well as its own celebrated brand of herb vinegars, mustards, preserves, and syrups for ice cream.

The West Tisbury Farmers' Market (tel: 693-0100) at the Old Agricultural Hall offers a wide variety of produce and prepared foods on Wednesdays (3–6pm) and Saturdays (9am to noon). The Takemmy Farm on State Road (tel: 693-1828) has also fresh fruits and vegetables and eggs sold on the honor system. For the sweet-tooth, try Chilmark Chocolates on South Road (tel: 645-3013).

Drinking on the Vineyard

Sometimes you bring your own

Inconvenient but true: on the Vineyard, alcohol is sold only in Oak Bluffs and Edgartown, which translates into a Bring-Your-Own policy throughout the rest of the island. In Oak Bluffs, Jim's Package Store (tel: 693-0263) offers the best selection of wine, beer and liquor on the Vineyard, along with the island's only commercial cigar humidor. Jim's has also been known to track down that particular single malt whiskey or merlot to suit the individual palate. Our Market (tel: 693-3000) in Oak Bluffs also special-orders wine and, in the fall, stocks the elusive Pumpkin Ale. Massachusetts law won't let you buy any of it on Sundays.

Restaurants
On Martha's Vineyard:

'Tonight we have…'

L'Etoile, at the Charlotte Inn in Edgartown, 27 S. Summer St, tel: 627-5187. Exquisite French dining for the sophisticated palate. $$$$

Beach Plum Inn, off North Road, between Menemsha Harbor and Menemsha Cross Road, in Menemsha, tel: 645-9454. Not to be confused with Nantucket's equally delightful Beach Plum Cafe, this unpretentious restaurant is all about serious Continental cuisine and breathtaking sunsets. A private vegetable garden and long-standing commitment to culinary excellence makes it worth the drive up-island. Reservations required. $$$$

Home Port, 512 North Road in Menemsha, tel: 645-2679. Super-fresh, busy and informal, with sit-down and take-out seafood for the impending sunset. Grab a bottle of wine down-island and head for the beach. $$$

The Black Dog Tavern, Beach Street Extension in Vineyard Haven, tel: 693-9223. Perhaps best known for its t-shirts, the Black Dog offers a daily-changing menu of traditional seafood, chowder and pasta with a view of the harbor. A breakfast favorite, especially among islanders in the winter months. $$$

Linda Jean's, 34 Circuit Avenue in Oak Bluffs, tel: 693-4093. Year-round favorite offering traditional American fare at down-to-earth prices. $$

Linda Jean's

Fresh Pasta Shoppe, 206 Main Street in Edgartown, tel: 627-5582. Quite simply the best pizza anywhere, according to islanders, and easily the most creative – try a slice of the Mexican, with a baked-bean base and sour cream, and take it out on the porch. $

On Nantucket:

The Straight Wharf Restaurant, Straight Wharf, off Main Street, tel: 228-4499. Weekly menu changes with two or three seatings nightly. Good seafood and lower-priced grill fare on the adjoining patio. $$$$

69

The Club Car, 1 Main Street, at Easy Street, tel: 228-1101. Once part of the Sconset train, the bar adjoins upscale dining ranging well beyond seafood – including veal, sirloin, lamb and a variety of international cuisine. $$$$

The Chanticleer Inn, 9 New Street, Siasconset, tel: 257-6231. Classical French cuisine offers world-class dining, with a $60 prix fixe and unparalleled wine cellar. Jacket required. Reservations required. $$$$

Beach Plum Cafe, 11 W. Creek Road, tel: 228-8839. Enchanting but small local favorite for inventive breakfasts, brunches, and dinners. No lunch in the summer. $$$

Obadiah's, 2 India Street, tel: 228-4439. Historic captain's house restored to offer straightforward seafood and generous portions of local specialties – served indoors or out – at reasonable prices. $$$

The Brotherhood of Thieves, 23 Broad Street, between Centre and Federal, no phone, no credit cards. 19th-century pub converted into islander-favorite, serving delicious burgers, chowder and curly fries by candlelight. $$

The Downy Flake, 6 Harbor View Way, at Children's Beach, tel: 228-4533. Homemade doughnuts, yummy pancakes and inexpensive take-out lunches. $

Active Vacations

Bikes for hire

Hiking, swimming, sailing, cycling and fishing – the islands not only anticipate outdoor activity but encourage it. Paved bicycle and in-line skating paths, well-marked walking trails and easy rental of bikes (both single and tandem) and mopeds are all ways of touring the islands without troubling to bring your own car over. What's more, you'll avoid a lot of parking headaches.

Exploring on foot, you'll discover inland wildlife missed by motor-traffic. On Martha's Vineyard, the Vineyard Conservation Society (tel: 693-9588) offers guided Winter Walks and periodic nature hikes through the island's wildlife refuge areas. On Nantucket, the Maria Mitchell Association's Natural Science Department (tel: 228-0898) organizes nature walks around the island, plus pamphlets for self-guided tours.

Both islands offer entire networks of paved bicycle paths, exclusively for cycling. There are good pocket-guides available at Mitchell's Book Corner in Nantucket and the Bunch of Grapes in Vineyard Haven describing the most popular bike routes. On the Vineyard, those who prefer to travel by horseback can call Scrubby Neck Stables in West Tisbury (tel: 693-3770) or Pond View Farm Riding Academy (tel: 693-2949).

Teeing off on Nantucket

Mild weather and open moors make the islands ideal for golfers, who report the Vineyard's nine-hole Mink Meadows Golf Course (tel: 693-0600) one of the best they've found. Nantucket offers two public courses, the Siasconset Golf Club (tel: 257-6596) and the Miacomet Golf Club on Hummock Pond Road (tel: 228-9764), plus the 18-hole Sankaty Head Golf Club (tel: 257-6391), which is private but open to the public in October. Both islands also have several public tennis courts. Stop by or call the Vineyard Chamber of Commerce (tel: 693-0085) or the Nantucket Chamber (tel: 228-1700) for locations and how to make reservations.

Shop for Nantucket 'Reds'

The islands' array of locally-made sweaters and scarves, pottery, basketry have made shopping another favorite pasttime. Once you maneuver past the t-shirt stands and mass-produced souvenirs, you'll find the shops of Nantucket's harborfront, Main Street in Vineyard Haven and throughout Edgartown and Oak Bluffs to be full of unique and well-crafted goods. For vintage tastes, check the local papers for ongoing flea markets, and stop in at the Book Den East in Oak Bluffs, one of the best stocked used-book stores in the Cape area.

Once you reach the waterfront, an entirely new landscape of possibilities opens. Sailboat rentals and instruction are offered throughout the summer by various charter services in the Nantucket Harbor and Vineyard Haven marina-area. Windsurfing instruction and rental is offered by Wind's Up (tel: 693-4252) on Martha's Vineyard.

Fishing, from surfcasting to charter excursions, continues to be one of the islands' most popular avocations. Bluefish and bonita, among others, can be found along the shore, while large game – swordfish, shark and bluefin tuna are favorites – await the offshore fisherman. If you're bringing your own boat to the islands, call the Nantucket dockmaster (tel: 228-1333) or the appropriate Vineyard Harbormaster (there are four, one for each harbor, so consult the Chamber's informative and free *Visitors' Guide*) for slip-rental information. Most slips have electrical hook-ups, and some also offer phone jacks, showers and laundry services.

Fishing tackle

Whale-watching excursions allow visitors a look at the beast whose pursuit, in many ways, shaped the islands into what they are today. Make reservations at Whale Watch Express on the Vineyard (tel: 800-576-6677) or Nantucket Whalewatch (tel: 800-322-0013). Rates typically run between $30–40 for adults, and around $20 for children.

Beaches

71

Swimmers and sunbathers will find ample beaches along these shorelines. Among the Vineyard's most popular beaches are State Beach, which stretches for 2 miles between Oak Bluffs and Edgartown facing Nantucket Sound, and Katama, the 3-mile public beach at South Beach in Edgartown. Up-island, facing Vineyard Sound, Lobsterville Beach in Gay Head offers a more pebbly beach with calmer water.

Katama and South Beach have lifeguards in occasional places, but none of the beaches have food or bathroom facilities. The water doesn't usually get warm enough for swimming until mid-July, but that doesn't stop sunbathers from venturing out earlier in search of a tan or social activity.

Lighthouse Beach, Edgartown

Nantucket offers seven public beaches, and some of the finest swimming and beachcombing in New England. In town, by the wharf, is Children's Beach, which offers bathrooms and food as well as lifeguards and a playground. Nearby Brant Point is out by the lighthouse at the mouth of the harbor. There are no facilities or lifeguards on duty here, and the ocean currents make swimming risky. Further along the north shore are Jetties Beach and Nantucket Sound Beach.

Other popular beaches include Surfside, on the island's south shore, and Codfish Park, the public beach in the fishing village of Siasconset ('Sconset') to the east. Nearly all of these beaches have lifeguards on duty, and the waves can stretch 5 to 6 feet high, easily high enough to surf in some areas.

Getting There

The ferry

By far the most popular way of getting to the islands, the 45-minute ferry ride to Martha's Vineyard leaves from the Steamship Authority in Woods Hole. The Nantucket trip takes about two and a half hours and leaves from Hyannis. Boats are equipped with snack bars which sell sandwiches, coffee, ice cream, and beverages including beer and wine. The boat schedule changes seasonally, so call (508) 477-8600 for Vineyard times and reservations, and (508) 540-2022 for Nantucket.

Vineyard Haven harbor

In the summer, several ferries carry passengers to Edgartown, Oak Bluffs and Vineyard Haven from Hyannis, Falmouth and New Bedford, but only the Steamship Authority carries cars. Call early (even months ahead) for car reservations. You won't need to book to walk on.

There are several ways of getting to the ferry:

By car

From Boston, take Route 3 south. For the Vineyard, cross the Cape Cod Canal on the Bourne Bridge, following the signs to Falmouth. For Nantucket, take the Sagamore Bridge across, then Route 6 to 132, following signs to Hyannis. On summer weekends, this may take two hours.

73

The classic approach

From New York, the drive may be six hours or more. Take I-95 to Providence, then I-195 east to the Cape. Cross on the Bourne Bridge and follow the rotary signs for either Falmouth or Hyannis, depending on your destination.

Coming in on the Massachusetts Turnpike from the west, you can exit onto 495 south (exit 11A) and circumnavigate the Boston area entirely. 495 becomes Route 25 and crosses over the Bourne Bridge.

By train and bus

From the north, west and south, Amtrak runs trains to Boston and Providence. Call (800) 872-7245 for schedules and fare information. Bonanza Bus Lines runs popular routes from Boston directly to the Steamship Authority in Woods Hole and Hyannis, and from Providence and New York to the south. Call (800) 556-3815.

Flying in

Both islands have year-round airports equipped for private and commercial flights. Cape Air (tel: 800-352-0714) has daily flights from Boston, New Bedford and Hyannis to both the Vineyard and Nantucket. Check with a travel agent or chamber of commerce for current information about flights from the New York area. For information about tie-downs for private planes, call the Vineyard's airport at 693-7022 or Nantucket's at 228-5300.

74

Over-sand permits on display

Wheels available

Getting Around

Should you bring your car over? Islanders will beg you not to – in the summer months, in-town congestion and an ongoing parking drought can quickly sour a pleasant morning – but it's really a question of the length of your stay and how much exploring you plan to do. On Nantucket, a single excursion out to Sconset beach certainly wouldn't justify bringing the car when you could take a shuttle-bus, but touring the island extensively may require something more robust than a bicycle.

The rental moped presents one compromise, although not necessarily the safest – moped aren't permitted on the paved bicycle paths and thus have to battle it out with cars on the narrow roads.

Driving

Off the beaten track, driving becomes an unfortunate necessity. Outside of their towns, both islands have networks of paved two-lane roads leading to practically every destination, though they're often narrow with little shoulder-space for pedestrians. Rolling hills and sharp corners sometimes occur in inconveniently scenic areas (such as the road leading up-island to Gay Head) so don't be afraid to pull off rather than getting distracted from the road.

Be patient: in summer, traffic may be severely backed up at one of the islands' many multi-entrance intersections (there are almost no traffic lights anywhere), and islanders in general aren't in any particular hurry. Taking in the landscape, slowing to wave at passing acquaintences or holding up traffic for a moment on Main Street to chat with a familiar face are all part of the island mentality.

In town, be aware of the marked one-way streets, which can prove frustrating at first. Foot traffic requires constant vigilance in the summer, when pedestrians often wander through the street with a kind of bovine indifference to on-coming traffic. Upon arriving to a specific town, it's usually easiest to find parking as soon as possible and continue on foot. Both the Vineyard and Nantucket offer some designated parking spots in town, and the sidestreets are clearly marked for two-hour parking or the appropriate regulation. Most hotels and inns provide guest parking, even in the middle of a fully developed block. Additionally, the Vineyard offers summer park-and-ride shuttles from outside of its main towns. In Edgartown, call 627-7448. For Vineyard Haven, call 627-7448. Park-and-ride shuttles usually leave every 10 minutes. Complimentary lift service is available for the disabled (tel: 693-4633).

Rental cars

Renting a car on the island is another alternative to bringing your own. In summer, reserve in advance.
On the Vineyard:
AAA Island Auto Rentals, 141 Main St., Edgartown, tel: 627-6800
Budget, Oak Bluffs, Vineyard Haven, Airport, 693-1911
Hertz, W. Tisbury Rd., Edgartown, tel: 627-4728
Vineyard Classic Cars, Lake St., Oak Bluffs, tel: 693-5551
On Nantucket:
Budget, Airport, tel: 228-5666
Hertz, Airport, tel: 228-9421
National, Airport, tel: 228-0300
Thrifty, Old South Rd., tel: 325-4610 or 800-367-2277

75

Shuttles and taxis

Both islands have regular shuttle bus services in summer. On Martha's Vineyard, M.V. Transportation Services (tel: 693-1589, 693-0058) runs a shuttle service around the island. Buses leave every half-hour or so in early summer, and every 15 minutes in July and August. Island tours are available from the steamship dock from spring to fall. Island tours usually last two and a half hours and cover all six towns, making one stop at the Gay Head cliffs. Taxis have pick-up areas at the dock, in the down-island towns and at the airport, and can pick up anywhere by request.

On Nantucket, Barrett's Tours (tel: 228-0174) offers service from their office on 20 Federal Street to such destinations as Jetties Beach, Surfside and Sconset. The buses usually run every half-hour, and the routes continue later in the evening on weekends. Several Nantucket companies also offer guided bus tours of the island. Taxis are readily available in town, at the Steamship Authority Terminal and in designated areas by the airport, and also pick up anywhere on the island, by arrangement. Call the Nantucket Chamber of Commerce (tel: 228-1700) for details.

Shuttle tours

Facts for the Visitor

Tourist information

The Martha's Vineyard Chamber of Commerce (tel: 693-0085) is on Beach Road in Vineyard Haven, across from the Post Office. It offers free maps, general information about the island, and a free 144-page Visitor's Guide.

The Nantucket Information Bureau (tel: 228-0925) is at 25 Federal Street, off Broad Street. In summer, offices open at the Steamship Wharf (tel: 228-0929), Straight Wharf (tel: 228-1929) and the airport (tel: 228-2115). The Chamber of Commerce (tel: 228-1700) is in the Pacific Club Building on Main Street.

Hospitals/health care

The Martha's Vineyard Hospital (tel: 693-0410) is on Linton Lane in Oak Bluffs. There is walk-in care service at Vineyard Medical Services Walk-In Care (tel: 693-6399). Leslie's (tel: 693-1010) on Main Street in Vineyard Haven is a full-service pharmacy with over-the-counter drugs.

Nantucket Cottage Hospital (tel: 228-1200) is at S. Prospect and Vesper Lane. Drug stores in town include Congdon's (tel: 228-0020) on Main Street and Island Pharmacy (tel: 228-6400) on Sparks Avenue.

Post offices

Martha's Vineyard has post offices in every town: at Beetlebung Corner in Chilmark (tel: 645-2535), on Edgartown-Vineyard Haven Road in Edgartown (tel: 627-7318), on Circuit Avenue in Oak Bluffs (tel: 693-1049), at Five Corners in Vineyard Haven (tel: 693-2815), and on State Road in West Tisbury (tel: 693-7899). There is also a Menemsha office (tel: 645-3501) and a West Chop branch at the general store on Franklin Street which are open in the summer months. Nantucket has two post offices, one on Federal Street in town (tel: 228-1067) and another in Siasconset (tel: 257-4402).

Churches

Both islands offer diverse religious services. On Martha's Vineyard, Catholic services are held at St Augustine's in Vineyard Haven and St Elizabeth's in Edgartown. Various Protestant denominations are represented in every town, and the Martha's Vineyard Hebrew Center holds services weekly. There are Quaker meetings, and a Jehovah's Witness Kingdom Hall in Vineyard Haven.

Nantucket has a variety of Protestant services, mainly in town. Catholic services are held at St Mary's Our Lady of the Isle, on Federal and Cambridge streets. Congregation Shirat HaYam offers pluralistic Jewish services at the Unitarian Church meeting house on Orange Street.

Activities For Children

Takemmy Farm

Both islands have a wide variety of children's activities, both indoors and out. On Martha's Vineyard, there are summer day-camps available on short-term basis. Fern & Feather, at the Felix Neck Wildlife Sanctuary (tel: 627-4850), the Children's Theatre Island Theatre Worshop (tel: 693-4060) and the Island Adventure Day Camp (tel: 693-1033, extension 156) are just a few of the possibilities. Sailing, swimming, tennis and golf instruction, as well as specific language, arts and sports camps, are available specifically for children – check with the Chamber for details. Adults and children together will enjoy visiting the llamas and miniature donkeys of Takemmy Farm in West Tisbury (tel: 693-2486) and, of course, the Flying Horses Carousel in Oak Bluffs (tel: 693-9481). Island theaters offer children's matinees at discounted prices year-round.

Here comes summer

On Nantucket, the Children's Beach offers safe, life-guard-supervised swimming, playground equipment and snacks. During Harborfest in July the beach becomes a center of children's activities and a parade. The Maria Mitchell Association offers several nature and astronomy programs for children throughout the summer. Call Loines Observatory at 228-9273 or the Association's Hinchman House at 228-0898 for details. The Nantucket Historical Association (tel: 228-1894) has information about an ongoing summer program allowing children to grind corn at the island's Old Mill, and bake fresh bread over an open fire at the Jethro Coffin House. On Wauwinet Road, the Nantucket Island School of Design and the Arts (tel: 228-9248) offers various art classes for children and adults, involving everything from clay and paint to performance pieces. There is a Saturday morning story hour at the Nantucket Library in the Atheneum on Lower India Street; call 228-1110 or 228-0666 for more information.

Charlotte Inn

Outermost Inn

Where to Stay

Book ahead in summer. The Steamship Authority terminal in Woods Hole has listings of hotels and vacancies. On Nantucket, the Chamber of Commerce keeps track of vacancies. Many hotels require a two-night minimum stay.

On the Vineyard
$$$$$
Charlotte Inn, S. Summer Street, Edgartown, tel: 627-4751; **Harbor View Hotel**, Starbuck Neck, Edgartown, tel: 627-7000; **Kelly House**, Kelly Street, Edgartown, tel: 627-7900; **Beach Plum Inn**, North Road, Menemsha, tel: 645-9454; **Outermost Inn**, Lighthouse Road, Gay Head, tel: 645-3511.

$$$$
Colonial Inn, N. Water Street, Edgartown, tel: 726-4711; **Edgartown Inn**, N. Water Street, Edgartown, tel: 627-4794; **Daggett House**, N. Water Street, Edgartown, tel: 627-4600; **Island Inn**, Beach Road, Oak Bluffs, tel: 693-2002; **Thorncroft Inn**, 278 Main Street, Vineyard Haven, tel: 693-3333; **Breakfast at Tiasquam**, Middle Road, Chilmark, tel: 645-3685.

$$$
Shiretown Inn, N. Water St., Edgartown, tel: 627-3353; **Wesley Hotel**, Lake Avenue, Oak Bluffs, tel: 693-6611; **Captain Dexter House**, 100 Main St., Vineyard Haven, tel: 693-6564; **Bayberry Inn**, Old Courthouse Road, West Tisbury, tel: 693-1984; **Lambert's Cove Inn**, Lambert's Cove Road, West Tisbury, tel: 693-2298.

$$
Heritage Hotel, Upper Main Street, Edgartown, 627-5161; **Dockside Inn**, Circuit Avenue Extension, Oak

Bluffs, tel: 693-2966; **Oak House**, Seaview and Pequot Avenue, Oak Bluffs, tel: 693-4187; **Tisbury Inn**, Main Street, Vineyard Haven, tel: 693-2200.

Youth hostel & campground

The Vineyard's youth hostel is on West Tisbury-Edgartown Road in West Tisbury. Cooking facilities and takes reservations. Price is about $13/night. (tel: 693-2665).

The Martha's Vineyard Family Campground, open from mid-May to October, is on the Edgartown-Vineyard Haven Road, about a mile from Vineyard Haven. It can take 180 vehicles and has a recreation hall and a store. Rates are $15/day for a campsite and $18/day for trailers, including hookup and water. No dogs or motorcycles. Call 693-3772 in season; (617) 784-3615 off-season.

On Nantucket

$$$$$

White Elephant, Easton Street, tel: 228-2500 or 800-IS-LANDS; **Wauwinet Inn**, Wauwinet Road, tel: 228-0145 or 800-426-8718; **Cliffside Beach Club**, Jefferson Avenue, tel: 228-0618; **White Elephant Hotel**, Easton and Williard Street, tel: 228-5500 or 800-475-2637.

$$$$

Jared Coffin House, 29 Broad Street, tel: 228-2400; **Westmoor Inn**, Westmoor Lane at Cliff Road, tel: 228-0877; **Harbor House**, 7 S. Beach Street, tel: 228-1500 or 800-475-2637; **Centerboard Guest House**, 8 Chester Street, between Centre and Easton, tel: 228-9696.

Jared Coffin house

$$$

Beachside Resort, 31 N. Beach Street at E. Lincoln, tel: 228-2241 or 800-322-4433; **Quaker House**, 5 Chestnut Street at Centre Street, tel: 228-0400; **Woodbox Inn**, Fair Street between Hiller and Darling Street, tel: 228-0587; **India House**, 37 India Street between Centre and Gardner, tel: 228-9043.

$$

Anchor Inn, 66 Centre Street, tel: 228-0072; **Martin House**, 61 Centre Street, tel: 228-0678; **Folger Hotel**, 89 Easton Street at North Avenue, tel: 228-0313 or 800-365-4371.

Youth hostel

At Surfside Beach, in an 1874 lifesaving station. Can hold between 50 and 70 overnighters with a three-night maximum. Rates are $10–15/night. Call 228-0433. There is no campground, and no camping – trailer, tent or otherwise – is allowed anywhere on the island. Fines are steep.

Nantucket's hostel

Index